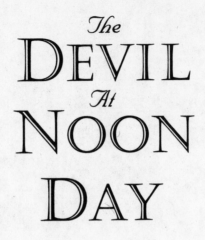

The
DEVIL
At
NOON
DAY

The DEVIL *At* NOON DAY

MAXIE DUNNAM

THOMAS NELSON PUBLISHERS
Nashville • Atlanta • London • Vancouver

Published in Nashville, Tennessee, by Thomas Nelson, Inc., Publishers, and distributed in Canada by Word Communications, Ltd., Richmond, British Columbia, and in the United Kingdom by Word (UK), Ltd., Milton Keynes, England.

Unless otherwise noted, all Scripture quotations are from THE NEW KING JAMES VERSION of the Bible, © 1979, 1980, 1982 by Thomas Nelson, Inc., Publishers.

Scripture quotations noted NRSV are from the NEW REVISED STANDARD VERSION of the Bible © 1989 by the Division of Christian Education of the National Council of the Churches of Christ in the U.S.A. All rights reserved.

Scripture quotations noted TLB are from *The Living Bible* (Wheaton, Illinois: Tyndale House Publishers, 1971) and are used by permission.

Scripture quotations noted NIV are taken from the HOLY BIBLE, NEW INTERNATIONAL VERSION ®. Copyright © 1973, 1978, 1984 by International Bible Society. Used by permission of Zondervan Bible Publishing House. All rights reserved.

The "NIV" and "New International Version" trademarks are registered in the United States Patent and Trademark Office by International Bible Society. Use of either trademark requires the permission of International Bible Society.

Scripture quotations noted NEB are from *The New English Bible*. Copyright © 1961, 1970 by the Delegates of the Oxford University Press and the Syndics of the Cambridge University Press. Reprinted by permission.

Scripture quotations noted PHILLIPS are from J. B. PHILLIPS: THE NEW TESTAMENT IN MODERN ENGLISH, Revised Edition. Copyright © J. B. Phillips 1958, 1960, 1972. Used by permission of Macmillan Publishing Co., Inc.

ISBN 0-7852-7876-1

Printed in the United States of America

To friends in other countries
whose lives dramatically witness to the truth:

"Greater is He that is within you
than he that is in the world."

Sundo and Kwan Soon Park Kim
Alan and Win Walker
Abel and Freda Hendricks
Olaf and Urve Parnamets
Manase and Losaline Tafea
Peter and Elizabeth Storey
Don and Bertha English

Contents

FOREWORD

As I began to read this book I was struck by the title of the opening chapter, "Is Your Devil Too Small?" My mind started reviewing various periods of my life when the size of my devil varied! For some strange reason, I went back to the very start of our ministry, when we served as missionaries in India from 1946 to 1962. For the first nine years we lived in a small town named Bidar, and I worked as an evangelist and church planter among primitive and rural people. The entire area was well known for its widespread belief in the practice of *bhanumathi*, a kind of animistic "black magic" that emphasized the power of evil spirits over almost every area of the people's lives. Most of their worldview and daily practices were based on placating these powerful and evil forces.

Many of the new converts had come out of this background, and even though their lives had been greatly changed by the transforming power of Christ, they continued to be influenced by their former beliefs. In my attempt to meet this challenge, I made a big mistake. Because I felt their devil was "too big," my first response was to present a devil who was "too small." So looking down my superior theological nose, I told them—poor ignorant and superstitious people—that they had nothing to fear; and I simply denied both the existence and power of such "spirits" with a kind of sarcastic humor. However, it didn't take long to discover that this approach didn't help them at all. Their encounters with powerful and bizarre forms of evil were just too prevalent and too real to be dismissed so casually. Isn't it amazing how many of us evangelicals deny in *pastoral practice* what we affirm in *theological teaching*! I was forced to go back to an in-depth study of the Scriptures and discovered that these simple people, in spite of some of their extravagant extremes, were much closer to the New Testament teachings than I was.

For the New Testament clearly teaches the reality of a personal Satan, evil spirits, and the nature of "spiritual warfare." Twenty-four out of twenty-nine times in the Gospels, Jesus addressed Satan as a person, and he is mentioned ninety times in the New Testament. According to Mark, the shortest Gospel, we find at least twelve references to a personified Satan or to demons. This means about one-third of Christ's ministry deals with the demonic. Matthew and Luke contain graphic eyewitness accounts of Jesus' battle against "evil" or "unclean" spirits. In Luke 4:16–27, Jesus, in His famous state-of-the-union address based on Isaiah 61, set forth His threefold mission of preaching, healing, and freeing the captives. In the book of Acts, Luke gave detailed experiences of how the early church carried out this mission. John described Jesus' mission as a confrontation with Satan and stated that the very purpose of His coming was "to destroy the works of the devil" (1 John 3:8). And the Epistles are filled with warnings of the cunning strategies of our personal adversary, the devil (1 Peter 5:8–9), and the spiritual armor necessary for our battle against "the cosmic powers of this present darkness" and the "spiritual forces of evil in the heavenly places" (Eph. 6:10–13).

But thank God it doesn't end there. The Scriptures boldly affirm that the death and resurrection of Jesus and His present power within us through the Holy Spirit *is greater than any and every spirit and assures us victory over them all!* This was precisely the message those oppressed people needed to hear. What a difference it made as it brought comfort, confidence, and courage to their formerly fear-filled lives.

I have always been grateful that, in the providence of God, it was the "foolish," the "weak," and the "lowly and despised in the world" (1 Cor. 1:27–28 NIV) who forced me to do my biblical homework and learn such important lessons early in my ministry. For soon after my time in India came years of ministry in the United States, with an emphasis on pastoral counseling. And although the location was on the other side of the globe, and the people were on the opposite side of the social and educational scale, the basic need and message remained exactly the same. For wherever we may be and whatever our ministry is, we need a truly biblical view of the devil that is neither too *big* nor too *small*.

These are the fundamental truths that Maxie Dunnam clearly proclaims in this book and attempts to keep in proper balance. Although he does not *major* on the more "exotic" or dramatic forms of spiritual warfare, he certainly does not relegate them to something *minor*, nor attempts to psychoanalyze them away. He gives many illustrations of sin, crime, and evil that cannot be explained apart from a demonic component. The devil is real, personal, and at work to tempt and destroy human lives today, even as "Satan entered into" Judas at the Last Supper (John 13:27). It was Abraham Lincoln who said, "The only common ground between good and evil is a battleground." Dr. Dunnam makes it clear that it is a *cosmic battleground*, between the "kingdom of God" and the "prince of darkness," in which eternal stakes are involved. Or in words similar to that which C. S. Lewis might use to express it, "Either God or Satan will eventually say, 'Mine' of everything and everyone that exists."

But the spectacular manifestations and battles with Satan are not the main thrust of the book. Rather, Dunnam issues a serious call to recognize the devil at work in what we would probably consider the unexceptional, everyday areas of life. Using the details of Jesus' three great temptations by Satan in the wilderness, the author brings out many important insights that help us relate our "ordinary" times of temptation to our Lord, who experienced the same basic spiritual assaults (Heb. 4:15). He points out that, because our devil is too small, we underestimate the terrible potential for evil when we consider certain issues as "trifles" or "no big deal." From his rich experiences as pastor and counselor he illustrates these temptations, which come from the daily round of ordinary life and cover a wide range of common "wilderness" experiences. They include our idolatrous highs of success and our depressive lows of loneliness and boredom; dealing with sexual desires; cutting corners on integrity; striving for self-esteem; overloading in order to prove ourselves; and being overcautious, which results in procrastination and the passion for security at any price. It is at these times when we need to be most on guard and realize our capacity to be deceived by the devil, whom Jesus described as a "liar and the father of lies" (John 8:44 NIV). Appropriate Scriptures are integrated with helpful psychological insights in order to help "deliver us from the evil one" (Matt. 6·13). Best of all is the constantly recurring theme that is found throughout the book: "He who is in you is greater than he who is in the world" (1 John 4:4).

It seems to me that both as individual Christians and as the Church, the body of Christ, we find ourselves with our backs against the wall. We face the power of evil on unprecedented scales, both in the lives of individuals and in social systems. In every evening news broadcast we see the devil at work in some unimaginable and shocking crime against innocent and helpless people, and we also see Satan in a gray flannel suit, operating through corporate and systemic evil. It's as if God is saying to His people today, "If you think that some new humanly conceived plan or program, some new humanly executed system, sermon, or service will turn things around, you are totally mistaken—dead wrong. Only when you *recognize* the cunning power of *Satan and the evil spirits you are up against*, and *realize* your own utter helplessness and *total dependence on My Holy Spirit*, only then will you be victorious."

An entry from John Wesley's journal (Monday, March 3, 1788) is a striking illustration of this. He was in Bristol, one of the three great centers of the slave trade, and had announced that he would preach Thursday evening on the subject of "Slavery."

In consequence of this . . . the house from end to end was filled with high and low, rich and poor . . . About the middle of the discourse, while there was on every side attention still as night, a vehement noise arose, none could tell why, and shot like lightning through the whole congregation. The terror and confusion were inexpressible. You might have imagined it was a city taken by storm. The people rushed upon each other with the utmost violence: the benches were broke in pieces and nine-tenths of the congregation appeared to be struck with the same panic. In about six minutes the storm ceased, almost as suddenly as it arose, and all being calm, I went on without the least interruption. It was the strangest incident of the kind I ever remember and I believe none can account for it without supposing some preternatural influence. Satan fought, lest his Kingdom should be delivered up. We set Friday apart as a day of fasting and prayer that God would remember these poor outcasts of men; and (what seems impossible with men, considering the wealth and power of their oppressors) make a way for them to escape and break chains in sunder.

Here is an amazing description of an encounter with a real devil, a presence of evil working at both the personal and societal level, plus the clear recognition for the necessity of the Holy Spirit's power through "fasting and prayer."

Martin Luther, in his great Reformation hymn, called Satan "The Prince of Darkness grim," affirmed that he is "still our ancient foe / [who] Doth seek to work us woe; / His craft and pow'r are great, / And, armed with cruel hate, / On earth is not his equal." I am grateful for those sections of the book in which Maxie Dunnam forces us to face these scriptural truths as he graphically takes us into the wilderness of Jesus' great temptations. But I am even more grateful for his final chapter in which he shows us how we can be joined with the victorious Christ as He saw Satan fall!

DR. DAVID A. SEAMANDS

Never Play Leapfrog
with a Unicorn

This is a book about the devil and demons; about temptation and exercising our spiritual muscle; about shunning, but also overcoming, temptation. It is about temptation as testing; the inevitability of failure, but also the sure victory that can be ours in Jesus Christ.

You may have heard it said that the devil's cleverest trick is to convince us that he does not exist. I believe that is true. So in the first three chapters we are going to focus on the reality of evil and the relentless presence of Satan. In these chapters we will look at temptation in general. Then in the remaining chapters, we will deal with temptation in specific areas of our lives.

You've heard the expression "Never play leapfrog with a unicorn." I doubt if anyone could miss the meaning of this vivid—we might say rather *pointed*—image. That maxim captures an underlying theme throughout this book: recognizing the power of evil and temptation in our lives, the danger that confronts us when we flirt with temptation or fail to recognize the presence of evil in the world. The ongoing warning is "Never play leapfrog with a unicorn." As vivid as that image is, it will become more real as we reflect on the demons in our lives, the temptations, and the testings that come daily.

This is also a book about spiritual warfare, but not in the sense of the numerous books that have been written during the past few years. I'm not dealing with the exotic but with the daily round of ordinary life, "the devil at noonday." In *Imitation of Christ* Thomas à Kempis said, "It is sometimes a very trifle, whence a great temptation arises."[1]

As prosaic and trifling as the circumstances and settings may be, the tempter's work in our life may be dramatic. I hope every reader will say "ummm . . . ," "yeah," and "I see." And I hope you will find here light to illuminate your way in whatever wilderness you confront Satan. I also hope you will be led to a greater confidence and certainty that "He who is in you is greater than he who is in the world" (1 John 4:4).

Is Your
Devil Too Small?

1

His name was Walker Railey. He was a charismatic young Dallas minister whose powerful sermons drew crowds to the First United Methodist Church. He had a lovely wife, two perfect children, and a brilliant future.

Then, on April 21, 1987, the week after Easter, Walker Railey found his wife, Peggy, lying unconscious on the floor of their garage. Someone had tried to strangle her. She never regained consciousness and remains in a vegetative state at the time of this writing.

Five years after that event, Walker Railey was indicted for attempting to murder his wife, but a jury found him not guilty.

A lot of strange circumstances surrounded the case, which planted huge questions about Walker Railey in the minds of many people.

Just before Easter, a couple of weeks before the attempt was made on his wife's life, Walker received threatening letters. One of those letters said, "Easter is when Christ arose, but you are going down." Walker preached that Easter Sunday wearing a bulletproof vest.

That letter, along with a couple of others, was produced on an old typewriter that was traced to a locked room in the church, and many people think Walker wrote the letters.

Walker also confessed to an affair with a Dallas psychologist, and he placed several phone calls to her on the night the attempt was made on Peggy's life.

Shortly after that violent event, Walker admitted himself into a hospital for treatment. Obviously considering suicide, he wrote a note that said, "There is a demon inside my soul. It has always been there. My demon tries to lead me down paths I do not want to follow. At times that demon has lured me into things I did not want to do."

It's a dramatic story. So many questions remain unanswered. So much mystery surrounds the case. It serves to introduce the subjects of this book: demons and the devil; temptation and exercising our spiritual muscle; shunning, but also overcoming temptation; the inevitability of failure; but, also, the sure victory that can be ours in Jesus Christ.

We begin where we have to begin if we are going to talk honestly about temptation: with the tempter himself—Satan.

Back in 1964, J. B. Phillips (of Bible translation fame) wrote a helpful little book titled *Your God Is Too Small*. He was on target. Our image of God is too small, far too small. We limit our spiritual growth and maturity because of our limited understanding of God.

But I've come to believe in the last few years that our image of the devil is also too small.

I heard of a young woman who announced to her mother that she had just broken off her engagement. "It's awful," she cried in tears. "I found out tonight that Kenneth does not believe in the devil. I just cannot go through with the wedding. I can't marry a guy who doesn't believe in the devil."

Her mother replied calmly, "That's all right, honey. You go ahead and marry Kenneth. We'll prove the devil to him!"

I don't know where you are in your belief and experience. I do know that the devil, sin, and temptation are a part of human experience. We need to clarify our thinking and, above all, equip ourselves to withstand what Scripture and Christian tradition call the "wiles of the devil."

Let's begin by positing some solid biblical truths.

The Devil Is Real

The witness of Scripture is clear. The three synoptic Gospels—Matthew, Mark, and Luke—all record the temptation experience of Jesus (Matt. 4:1–11; Mark 1:12–13; Luke 4:2–13). Satan made a bold attempt to divert the Son of God from His divine mission. Apparently the attacks did not surprise Jesus, and, intriguingly, the Temptation was not outside God's direct leading. In each Gospel account, it was the Holy Spirit who led Jesus into the wilderness, where the Temptation took place.

3

The account is familiar to those who study the New Testament. Jesus, preparing for His public ministry, went into the wilderness to fast and pray. When He had fasted forty days, the devil made his move. He sought to take advantage of Jesus' weak physical condition, to divert Him from His messianic call, and to test His devotion to the Father.

Immediately we see how cunning the devil is. He first tempted Jesus where He was most vulnerable—His *hunger*. Satan urged Jesus to use His divine powers to obtain food by turning stones into bread. Jesus fought back by citing a passage from the Old Testament: "Man shall not live by bread alone" (Deut. 8:3). This confirmed there in the wilderness what would be demonstrated over and over again in Jesus' life and ministry: His total commitment and dependence on the Father.

His attempt at physical temptation repulsed, the devil took another route: fallen humanity's desire for power. He offered Jesus the kingdoms of the world and their splendor in return for His obeisance and worship. Jesus knew the story of His people, Israel. Again and again they had succumbed to this temptation, forsaking God and worshiping foreign gods. Again, He repulsed the enemy, confirming His intense devotion to God alone by citing another Old Testament text: "Fear the LORD your God and serve Him" (Deut. 6:13).

Not outdone yet, the devil took a third approach. He tempted Jesus to test God's devotion to Him. Matthew 4:5–6 tells us that he challenged Jesus to jump from a high precipice and force God to rescue Him. Again, see the devil's cunning. He himself quoted Scripture, reminding Jesus of the divine promise that He would never be harmed: "He shall give his angels charge over you, / To keep you in all your ways. / In their hands they shall bear you up, / Lest you dash your foot against a stone" (Ps. 91:11–12).

Jesus' relationship to the Father, a relationship of trust, needed no test. Jesus expressed His unshakable trust by recalling God's written revelation of His will. He verbalized God's command: "You shall not tempt the LORD your God" (Deut. 6:16).

This interchange was more than a battle of words, though we need to learn that immersing our minds and hearts in God's Word and claiming it as our *sword* is one of our most effective weapons in battling the devil and temptation. This was a battle of will and heart, of devotion and life. Jesus was victorious in the battle, and the devil left Him. Then later, Jesus could witness to His disciples, proclaiming, "The ruler of this world . . . has nothing in Me. But that the world may know that I love the Father, and as the Father gave Me commandment, so I do" (John 14:30–31).

A close look at these temptations reveals that they are representative. The whole range of human nature—our drives, our desires, and our search for meaning—is addressed. Talking about the risen, ascended Christ, the writer of Hebrews told us we have "a High Priest who . . . was in all points tempted as we are, yet without sin" (Heb. 4:15). This does not mean that Jesus experienced and overcame every specific temptation suffered by humankind through the ages. It does mean that the temptation experience of Jesus in the wilderness is representative of every facet of human nature through which Satan assails us. It also means that we have a Savior who not only loves us, but loves us as One who knows us, who lived our lives, who faced the temptations we face, and who overcame them.

We will look more closely at each of these temptations in later chapters. For now we are reiterating a truth about which Scripture is very clear: The devil is real. To underscore that reality, ask yourself this question: Where did this narrative of Jesus' temptation come from? It had to have come from the lips of our Lord Himself. No one was there to witness His great struggle; therefore, we have to conclude that Jesus shared this profound experience out of His own spiritual life, and the Gospel writers recorded it.

We will come back to this later, but we need to note it now to keep perspective. Matthew, Mark, and Luke—who recorded the story of Jesus' temptation—said that it happened immediately after Jesus' baptism. In Matthew, chapter 3 closed with the record of that baptism:

When He had been baptized, Jesus came up immediately from the water; and behold, the heavens were opened to Him, and He saw the Spirit of God descending like a dove and alighting upon Him. And suddenly a voice came from heaven, saying, "This is My beloved Son, in whom I am well pleased." (vv. 16–17)

Chapter 4 opens with this: "Then Jesus was led up by the Spirit into the wilderness to be tempted by the devil." From Jesus' experience, we can derive two truths for our lives. One, the wilderness of temptation is as much a part of the landscape of the Christian life as the River Jordan is of affirmation. Two, life for the Christian is a Spirit-led journey.

What a picture! Immediately after being affirmed as God's Beloved Son, Jesus is led by the Spirit into the wilderness and is tempted by the devil. Jesus was being pressed irresistibly by a knowledge that there was something that had to be done there, a battle that had to be fought. From the beginning the Gospel writers make it clear that this conflict with Satan is neither incidental nor accidental. The Spirit led Jesus into the wilderness to challenge Satan. This was the initial and representative engagement, confirming the mission of Jesus to "destroy the works of the devil" (1 John 3:8).

It's not only here in this record of the temptation of Jesus that the Bible presents the fact of Satan, but in account after account, the Scripture asserts his reality. Though Scripture has little to say about the origin of the devil and evil, it is replete with stories in which powerful forces of evil are recognized and dealt with. Perhaps the most dramatic story in the Old Testament is that of Job.

The book of Job records how God and Satan fought for the soul of one person. Job is one of the oldest books of the Bible, and it is here that Satan's name is mentioned for the first time (Job 1:6). The literal meaning of the name *Satan* is "adversary."

Satan sneeringly suggested that Job's faith was dependent on his prosperity, on God's preferential treatment. God granted him the power to test Job, and the devil went to work. Job was subjected to loss after loss and every form of suffering, yet he remained loyal and faithful to God.

Satan's confession in Job 1:7 is a useful expression of his reality and occupation. He roams about the earth with the evil purpose of separating persons from God.

The devil is real. Paul sounds the warning clearly. He calls Satan "the Prince of Darkness." He called on the Ephesians to put on the whole armor of God and prepare themselves for battle. He wrote,

> *For we do not wrestle against flesh and blood, but against principalities, against powers, against the rulers of the darkness of this age, against spiritual hosts of wickedness in the heavenly places. (Eph. 6:12)*

This may be the most dramatic and familiar word of Paul concerning the reality of evil, the devil, and demonic powers. But it is not an isolated expression. The following words of Paul also are found in the New Testament:

> *For I am persuaded that neither death nor life, nor angels nor principalities, nor powers, nor things present nor things to come, nor height nor depth, nor any other created thing, shall be able to separate us from the love of God which is in Christ Jesus our Lord. (Rom. 8:38–39)*

> *Then comes the end, when He delivers the kingdom to God the Father, when He puts an end to all rule and all authority and power. For He must reign till He has put all enemies under His feet. (1 Cor. 15:24–25)*

> *. . . which He worked in Christ when He raised Him from the dead and seated Him at His right hand in the heavenly places, far above all principality and power and might and dominion, and every name that is named, not only in this age but also in that which is to come. (Eph. 1:20–21)*

> *And you He made alive, who were dead in trespasses and sins, in which you once walked according to the course of this world, according to the prince of the power of the air, the spirit who now works in the sons of disobedience, among whom also we all once conducted ourselves in the*

lusts of our flesh, fulfilling the desires of the flesh and of the mind, and were by nature children of wrath, just as the others. (Eph. 2:1–3)

His intent was that now, through the church, the manifold wisdom of God should be made known to the rulers and authorities in the heavenly realms. (Eph. 3:10 NIV*)*

And having disarmed the powers and authorities, he made a public spectacle of them, triumphing over them by the cross. (Col. 2:15 NIV*)*

In 1979, I wrote a commentary on the book of Ephesians. My son Kevin was then twelve years old. This is a part of what I wrote:

Paul's words about wrestling "against principalities, against powers, against the rulers of the darkness of this age, against spiritual hosts of wickedness in the heavenly places" (Eph. 6:12) do not strike Kevin's ears with strangeness. Nor mine. Kevin trembles in the presence of the evil of a chaotic world that is going mad and is seemingly bent on its own destruction. One day, if we escape the portended atomic nightmare, Kevin will tremble as surely as he recognizes evil expressing itself within himself—in those dark nights of his soul when opposing powers will pull him with person-rending might in opposite directions. Already he has hints of the working of those powers as his sexual passions become more intense, as he wrestles with the "easy" way of cheating rather than studying for good grades, as he sorts out his instincts and drives, his needs for affirmation and acceptance.

At least by hint, Kevin knows what most of us have discovered, that Paul was writing of forces which invade the world, our inner and interpersonal worlds, to make us sin, even to destroy us. So we must be strong in the Lord. To be so requires putting on the whole armor of God.[1]

The devil is real. What Kevin at age twelve knew "at least by hint," he was to discover in its full power as he wrestled with drugs and alcohol. I will never forget a midnight call when he was nineteen. He was in a restaurant/bar in Memphis. When he told me where he was, I knew he was in trouble. His words underscored the fact. "Please come get me," he said. "The devil is here, and I can't get free."

I went, and he was right. I could feel the darkness of evil in that shadowy place. The devil is real.

The Devil Is a Personal Power

I used to refrain from being so explicit about this. I'm not sure why. Maybe I was intimidated by so-called liberal theology that relegated the notion of demons and Satan himself to a worldview that did not harmonize with modern scientific understanding. This theology said that the notion of the devil and demons was just a relic from a prescientific worldview. Until the Enlightenment (1650–1780), belief in a personal devil and his minions was all but universal. But people of the Enlightenment couldn't believe in that sort of thing.

But think for a moment about the Enlightenment. When the so-called Age of Enlightenment began, we thought the Dark Ages were over, that the light of human reason would push back the darkness and we would live in the light of a fully blossomed civilization.

We began the twentieth century as people of the Enlightenment, confident that we would see the full flowering of humanity. We would live rationally. Utopias would be constructed through scientific planning. With the technology that was available to us, we would see a time when life would be free of pain and misery. The Enlightenment was coming to full flower, and we were reaping the harvest of at least one hundred years of science.

But here we are, in the last decade of the twentieth century. How do we now assess this century? It has been the most devastating century in the history of humanity. More people have been killed through wars and through the inhumanity of man than ever before. The great powers that were going to usher in a perfect world have been used to kill and enslave millions and to make the world more dangerous than ever.

And so, today, people with scientific credentials—not crazed preachers breathing hellfire like David Koresh of the Branch Davidians in Texas, but rational men and women of science—are among those who are suggesting that there is something like evil after all. If we remain vigilant and if we are aware of its power, we may be able to hold it in check, but we are not able to eliminate it.

So, whatever timidity I have had in talking about the reality of evil and the fact that the devil is real is gone. As I have witnessed the power of sin and evil, and as I have sought to be faithful to Scripture, my timidity has dissolved. In the Christian view of reality, we trust Scripture as divine revelation. As author J. Oswald Sanders reminded us, "Where Scripture is silent, or speaks with reserve, the expositor will do well to advance only tentative opinions. But where Scripture has spoken clearly, we have heard all we need to know, and our opinions need not be tentative."[2]

So I'm going to be dogmatic. Satan is not merely an evil influence; he is a personal power.

Go back to Walker Railey. During his days of ministry at First United Methodist Church in Dallas, I received transcripts of his sermons. He was a powerful preacher. I still have some of those sermons in my files. In one of those sermons (preached on February 24, 1985, two years before his wife's attempted murder), he said, "Satan is . . . simply a symbolic way of confronting us with a continuing experience of evil in human affairs."

I wonder what Walker Railey would say about that conclusion now? Something obviously changed. His suicide note went far beyond an expression of Satan as simply symbolic of evil. He said there is a "demon inside my soul."

When you read Scripture carefully, you come to the realization that the word *devil* is never used to personify evil in man or the world but to signify an evil, personal spirit. The Gospels show that the evil one was a personal devil whom Jesus met in the wilderness.

Your devil is too small if you do not accept the fact that the devil is real and that the devil is a personal power.

It would be hard to convince Jesus, and ever so difficult to convince those Gospel writers who retold the account they had heard from Him, that the tempter in the wilderness was just "an inclination in you and me," just a symbol of the presence of evil in the world.

The devil is real, and the devil is a personal power.

The Devil Wants to Control Your Life

Now, here's a third fact: The devil wants to control your life. Indeed, he will control your life if you allow him.

Every now and then a person will ask me, "Have you ever confronted someone who was demon-possessed?" I used to say no to that.

But I don't answer that way anymore. The question is not whether someone is demon-possessed or not. It's a question of the degree—the degree to which God is in control or out of control of our lives. And don't we have to ask the question, who is it, or what is it that is controlling my life? In Ephesians 4:27, Paul admonished us not to "give place to the devil." This is the closest Paul came to a discussion of demon-possession in his letters. Yet we know from Luke's account in the book of Acts that Paul engaged in the casting out of evil spirits. So when he urges the Christians to whom he is writing in Ephesus not to allow the devil a place or foothold, he is warning against the possibility of our relinquishing even partial control of our lives to the devil. It follows that, in Paul's mind, the devil can make significant inroads even in a Christian's life.

Back in 1983, M. Scott Peck, psychiatrist and author of an earlier best-selling book *The Road Less Traveled*, wrote a disturbing but helpful book titled *People of the Lie*. The subtitle was *The Hope for Healing Human Evil*. In his introduction he confessed trepidation in view of the book's potential for harm, the pain it would cause some readers, and the possibility that some readers might use the book's information to harm others. "This is not a nice book," he wrote. "It is about our dark side, and in large part about the very darkest members of our human community—those I frankly judge to be evil."[3] Peck argued that psychiatry must recognize evil as an identifiable psychological state that can be dealt with

15

only by recognizing and naming it for what it is. As an open-minded scientist (his self-description) he came to believe in the reality of the devil and in the reality of devil possession, though he believed possession was a rare phenomenon.

You may think yourself too rational, too modern, too sophisticated to talk about demon possession. Read your newspaper and watch television. When I began writing this book, three teenage boys were in jail in West Memphis. They were accused and later convicted of brutalizing and killing three little boys. There were strong indications that these teenagers were involved in devil worship. Reporting on this, *The Commercial Appeal*, a Memphis newspaper, put it in the context of similar cases.

Carl Raschke, a religious studies professor, is the author of *Painted Black*, a 1990 book about satanic-related crimes, including several homicides in North America.

Steven Newberry of Joplin, Missouri, for instance, died at the hands of Satan-worshiping high school buddies in 1987 in a case Raschke says strongly resembles the publicly known details of the West Memphis case.

Mark Kilroy, a University of Texas premed student never made it back from a 1989 spring break trip to the Mexican border town of Matamoros. He was killed by drug smugglers who thought sacrifices would convince Satan to protect them from the police.

In Lonoke, Arkansas, last year, a 31-year-old man and two teenagers were convicted in the ritualistic knife slaying of a 14-year-old girl in a cemetery there.

"The truth of the matter is that satanic crimes in this country are definitely out there," Raschke said, "even though there are some people who just don't want to believe it."[4]

Scott Peck in his book *People of the Lie* described a person possessed by a demon:

When the demonic finally spoke clearly in one case, an expression appeared on the patient's face that could be described only as Satanic. It was an incredibly contemptuous grin of utter hostile malevolence. . . . The eyes were hooded with lazy, reptilian torpor . . . open wide with blazing hatred.[5]

The demonic, more often than not, is not spectacular. As Lewis Smedes said,

Satan is no fool. Getting a poor devil to roll his eyes and make a gargoyle of his face is not a demonic triumph. Get an ordinary person committed sober-faced to an uplifting, inspiring lie, however, and you have gotten yourself a prize—if you happen to be a demon.[6]

I am seeking to make the case that the devil is real and wants to control your life. Just for a moment, lay aside your modern sophistication and release your preconceptions and your prejudices. Can you convincingly refute the argument that there is a mysterious force in us, something alien to our better selves, something that if given free rein would slowly, systematically, ruin our lives?

When I talk to people who are recovering from addictions, or who have not yet moved into recovery, the statement I hear more often than not is this: "I'm losing everything because of my addiction, but I can't seem to do anything about it."

Call it what you will, but don't fail to recognize and acknowledge the fact that there is something in us and outside us, something present in the world that is against us—a force that, unresisted, will ruin our lives.

So I restate the point: The devil wants to control our lives, and he will control our lives if we let him.

You can read all the self-help books in the world, and they will not show you how to do battle with the evil one who wants to control your life. These books may tell you that you can solve your problems with more enthusiasm, more willpower, more positive thinking, more ambition. But there is one huge flaw in all these prescriptions. They are based on the assumption that we are rational creatures who simply need to find the right technique to live successfully, that all we need is to identify the right idea—and to put it into practice.

But it doesn't work because the devil is real.

In the next chapters, we will explore the dynamics of sin and evil and temptation in our lives.

But let me close this chapter by underscoring an encouraging fact that will be reiterated throughout this book: As real as the devil may be, as committed as he may be to controlling your life, *his power is limited.* He is no match for the indwelling Christ. The record of Jesus' battle with the devil in the wilderness showed us that "Christ at His lowest, vanquished the devil at his highest; the Savior at His weakest, routed His (adversary) at his strongest."[7]

The witness of Scripture is this: "Greater is He that is within you, than he that is in the world." This is not only the witness of Scripture, it's the witness of Christians throughout the ages. Though there is an ongoing battle that we fight with the tempter and all of temptation, the decisive battle has been won. Jesus died on the cross. God raised Him from the dead. The Holy Spirit was given as an advocate for Christ on our behalf. So Christ lives in us. That means that the living Christ joins us in battle against all that would destroy us and prevent us from being less than what God calls us to be. And Christ will win.

The Wilderness:
A Place of Testing

2

The setting for Jesus' temptation was the wilderness. Jesus had just been baptized in the River Jordan, and Scripture says, "Immediately the Spirit drove Him into the wilderness. And He was there in the wilderness forty days, tempted by Satan, and was with the wild beasts; and the angels ministered to Him" (Mark 1:12–13).

Between the Jordan and Jerusalem, there is a large wilderness area of jagged and warped landscape. I've been there. It is a barren place. The hills to the south of it run right out to the edge of the Dead Sea and drop straight down twelve hundred feet into one of the lowest spots on earth. It is a desolate place of intense heat and emptiness.

It was in that wilderness, in company with wild beasts, that Jesus spent forty days fasting and praying and, later, being tempted by Satan.

But where this wilderness was, and its landscape, is not important. A specific geographical wilderness is not what begs our attention in this chapter, but the wilderness as a backdrop, a setting for our struggle with Satan, with temptation— our struggle to be in tune with and committed to God.

Loren Eisley, in his book *The Unexpected Universe*, tells of a wilderness experience. One night the train on which he was riding was stalled in a marsh outside the city. A kind of flame-wreathed landscape attended by shadowy figures could be glimpsed from the window.

After a time he and a companion got off the train and strolled forward to explore the curious sight. It turned out that what they were looking at was the smoke and the dull embers of the burning city dump. This smoke and smoldering flame created strange shadows and sent choking vapors into the sky. The experience was made more eerie in that there were people, some workers, others scavengers, who were forking over the rubbish.

Eisley said that for a moment he had the feeling that must exist on the borders of hell, "Where everything, wavering among heat waves, is transported to another dimension. One could imagine ragged and distorted souls grubbed over by scavengers for what might usefully survive."

He stood in silence, watching this grim, great burning. He saw sodden papers that had been forked into the flames. He thought to himself, *Perhaps this is the place where last year's lace valentines had gone, along with old Christmas trees, and the beds I had slept on in childhood.*

"I suppose you get everything here," he said to the grimy attendant. The fellow nodded indifferently, drew a heavy

22

glove across his face, and in a deep reflective mood said, "Know what?"

"No," Eisley confessed.

"Babies . . . ," the man growled, ". . . even dead babies sometimes turn up. From there." He gestured contemptuously toward the city.

The engine bell sounded and Eisley had to reboard the train. He made a parting gesture of good-bye as around him the gloom and dark shapes worked ceaselessly at the dampened fires.

"We get it all," the dump philosopher repeated. "Just give it time to travel, we get it all."[1]

That was a wilderness experience for Loren Eisley. It set him thinking about his own life, his history, about humankind and the tragic and glorious dimensions of our story.

So the wilderness doesn't have to be a specific geographical place. It is the wilderness as a symbol and metaphor that begs our attention as we think about Jesus' temptation and our own.

I have counseled with many Christians in distress as they battle temptation. They question themselves and their spiritual maturity. "Will I never reach a point beyond temptation?" they ask. I remind them of Jesus' struggle. He did not drive the tempter away forever in that dramatic battle in the wilderness. Though He never stepped out of the will of God, Jesus was not free of temptation. As He hung on the cross, the watching crowd taunted Him, echoing the words of

Satan, "If You are the Son of God, prove Your-self." Among themselves they sneered, "He saved others; let Him save Himself if He is the Christ, the chosen of God" (Luke 23:35).

If you were dying such a ghastly death and had the power to save yourself, it would be no small temptation to do so. In some of His last words Jesus reminded the disciples of their share and support in His ministry: "But you are those who have continued with Me in My trials" (Luke 22:28). We fool ourselves when we assume that mature Christians are immune to temptation and the visitation of Satan. We will look at this issue more specifically in the next chapter.

We also set ourselves up for frustration and guilt when we believe that the temptation we are experiencing is peculiar to us, or that there must be some answers, some solutions that we have missed. Jesus never evaded the tempter. Who are we to think we might?

In Chapters 4, 5, and 6, we will look at each of the specific temptations of Jesus in the wilderness. In this chapter we will focus on the wilderness itself, as a metaphor for temptation.

The Wilderness Speaks of Struggle and Testing

Let's begin in our thinking with this: The wilderness is a metaphor for struggle and testing. It speaks of the struggle between light and darkness, life and death.

The philosopher George Santayana said, "Life is not a spectacle or a feast; it is a predicament."[2] We can identify with that, can't we? Our lives are punctuated by one struggle after another. *Predicament* is a good word to describe where we are much of the time. *Suffering* is another. One of the most dramatic expressions of this in Scripture is Paul's confession in Romans:

> *For as many as are led by the Spirit of God, these are sons of God. For you did not receive the spirit of bondage again to fear, but you received the Spirit of adoption by whom we cry out, "Abba, Father." The Spirit Himself bears witness with our spirit that we are children of God, and if children, then heirs—heirs of God and joint heirs with Christ, if indeed we suffer with Him, that we may also be glorified together. For I consider that the sufferings of this present time are not worthy to be compared with the glory which shall be revealed in us. For the earnest expectation of the creation eagerly waits for the revealing of the sons of God. (8:14–19)*

When we are reflective, many of us would confess with Paul that we struggle with sin and evil—wicked thoughts, destructive leanings, unhealthy desires.

Sometimes these thoughts and leanings and desires are translated into action—destructive action. It is as though we are not in control. And we're filled with questions:

- What gets into people?
- What drives human beings into destructive and brutal acts?
- What prompts us to pursue a collision course of self-destruction?
- What drives people to drug addiction and alcoholism?
- Where do monstrous atrocities like the Holocaust come from?
- How does one explain the dark, wild, mean, and ugly underside of human personality?

Some folks say, "The devil made me do it." A little girl got fed up with her baby brother one day. She pushed him down, called him a name, and then spit on him. Her father scolded her and said, "Honey, I think the devil made you do that." The little girl answered, "The devil might have made me push him down and call him names, but I thought of spitting on him all by myself!"

In New Testament times people believed that most sickness and all mental illness were caused by demons, by evil spirits that attacked and sometimes inhabited human beings. Demons were numerous and much to be feared.

Since the first century specific causes have been found for many ills once attributed to demons. However, still today, many people who work most closely with human ills do not belittle the power of the demonic, of evil, in human life. Paul Tournier in *A Doctor's Casebook* writes, "Doubtless there are many doctors who in their struggle against disease have had, like me, the feeling that they were confronting, not something passive, but a clever and resourceful enemy.". . .

People addicted to drugs, alcohol, tobacco, and the misuse of food, as well as those engaged in other kinds of compulsive and self-destructive behavior, often feel possessed, divided against themselves, unable to explain or control their actions. The way they feel and the way they explain their feelings is often not far removed from first-century descriptions of demon possession.[3]

Scott Peck in his book *People of the Lie* sought to deal with the subject of evil. His eight-year-old son gave him a workable definition. The little boy said, "Why, Daddy, *evil* is 'live' spelled backward." I don't know how a mere child could have that kind of insight, but it is perceptive, isn't it? *Live* spelled backward is *evil*. Dr. Peck concluded that *evil* is not only the opposite of *live*, it is in opposition to life.[4] Evil is that which opposes life and can destroy life.

In his book, Dr. Peck assumes a rather radical position. He says that most of us would be what he calls "people of the lie." Ordinary people—the educated as well as the uneducated, the rich as well as the poor, and ordinary, solid citizens like Sunday school teachers, bankers, and, yes, even preachers!

"People of the lie" are ordinary people who live out their days denying the evil that is within them. They are blind to the struggle that is happening, unaware that the struggle is a life-and-death battle of good against evil. And Dr. Peck makes the point that the denial of the demonic within us causes us to live a lie. He concludes that the only way a person can be restored is to have the evil spirit evicted. That's what Jesus would say. His was a ministry of casting out demons, freeing people of the evil thoughts, destructive leanings, and dark passions that controlled their lives; Jesus gave them the direction and the power to engage in that struggle and emerge triumphant. Mark's Gospel had hardly begun before he was recording instances of Jesus' dealing with demons in the lives of others. In the first twenty verses of his Gospel, Mark recorded Jesus' baptism by John the Baptist, His battle with Satan in the wilderness, and His call of the disciples. With verse 21, Mark registered the beginning of Jesus' public ministry, and immediately there was an encounter with a person with an "unclean spirit."

Then they went into Capernaum, and immediately on the Sabbath He entered the synagogue and taught. And they were astonished at His teaching, for He taught them as one having authority, and not as the scribes. Now there was a man in their synagogue with an unclean spirit. And he cried out, saying, "Let us alone! What have we to do with You, Jesus of Nazareth? Did You come to destroy us? I know who You are—the Holy One of God!" But Jesus rebuked him, saying, "Be quiet, and come out of him!" And when the unclean spirit had convulsed him and cried out with a loud voice, he came out of him. Then they were all amazed, so that they questioned among themselves, saying, "What is this? What new doctrine is this? For with authority He commands even the unclean spirits, and they obey Him." And immediately His fame spread throughout all the region around Galilee. (Mark 1:21–28)

We don't know whether this man had heard Jesus preach before or if he simply happened to be in the crowd that day. The other worshipers were not aware of the civil war that was going on inside him, unaware that here was a person fighting for his very life, about to be drowned in a sea of forces beyond his control.

This needy, demon-filled man had a *double consciousness*. His humanity desperately drew him to Jesus—pulled him almost irresistibly. But there was evil in him also. There was the demonic, which was repelled by Jesus.

Isn't that like most of us? We're drawn to Christ in our deepest longing. We know that there is healing and cleansing in Jesus. But other forces pull us away from Jesus and from drawing close to Him.

The Wilderness Speaks of Solitude and Solitude Is a Time of Testing

The wilderness also speaks of solitude, and solitude can be a time of testing. In solitude we may experience our fiercest testing, our worst defeats, and our greatest victories.

Jesus' experience in the Garden of Gethsemane is a dramatic picture of this (see Luke 22:39–48). It is interesting that Luke begins his account of this experience with Jesus' admonition to His disciples, "Pray that you may not enter into temptation." When He left them and went farther into the garden for solitude and prayer, He experienced one of His greatest temptations and struggles. It's easy to romanticize that night and miss the fact that this was a time and place of a deeply troubling ordeal. So intense was the struggle that not only did Jesus break out in a sweat of tension and stress, but the sweat was "like great drops of blood falling down to the ground" (Luke 22:44).

Another kind of temptation awaited the disciples. Jesus' concern that they enter not into temptation proved well founded. His enemies, led by Judas, came to get Him, armed and ready for resistance. The disciples asked, "Lord, shall we strike with the sword?" (Luke 22:49). Matthew's Gospel records Jesus' response: "Put your sword in its place, for all who take the sword will perish by the sword" (Matt. 26:52).

Jesus experienced a fierce testing, but He won a great victory: "Not as I will, but as You will" (Matt. 26:39). So with us. Solitude is often a time of testing.

Martin Buber, the great Jewish philosopher, was once asked a series of grandiose sounding questions by members of an audience to whom he had lectured. Finally he burst out, "Why don't we ask each other the questions that come to us at three o'clock in the morning as we are tossing on our beds?" The American philosopher Thoreau contended that we learn more about ourselves in a sleepless night than on a trip to Europe.

The wilderness suggests solitude. Solitude, whether chosen or forced upon us, can be a time of testing. In solitude we often are forced to examine our values and priorities.

That's what was going on with Jesus in His wilderness experience. He spent forty days in solitude. What was He doing? He was making final preparation for His public ministry. He wrestled with the devil in a life-and-death struggle. His identity and the shape of His ministry were beaten out on the anvil of temptation. Three times the devil tempted Jesus to accept the role of a popular, power-wielding Messiah. Three times Jesus refused. His testing did not end there in the wilderness. Luke's account of this temptation experience closes as follows: "Now when the devil had ended every temptation, he departed from Him until an opportune time" (Luke 4:13). The King James Version translates that the devil "departed from Him for a season."

The wilderness speaks of solitude, and solitude is a time of testing.

I know a young minister who violated his marriage vows of fidelity. In solitude, he was convicted and led to confession and reconciliation with his wife.

I know couples in the congregations I have served whose marriages are threatened because of adultery. These people are not going to be able to live with this lie. They will be tested in their solitude.

Solitude is often forced on us by illness. Flannery O'Connor, from Millegeville, Georgia, was one of our great contemporary Southern writers. She was a Roman Catholic and an ardent Christian. She used her fiction as a vehicle for the expression of her faith.

O'Connor was sick most of her life, but she rarely mentioned sickness or suffering. On one occasion she did mention it, and what she said is instructive. "I've never been anywhere but sick. In a sense, sickness is a place . . . where there is no company, where nobody can follow. Sickness before death is a very appropriate thing and I think those who don't have it miss one of God's greatest mercies."[5]

That's a tough but instructive insight. Have you ever thought of sickness in that fashion? "Sickness is a place." What does she mean by that? Sickness is something that happens to you, but it is more. When we are sick we are driven to think deeply, to feel beyond ourselves, to identify with the suffering of others, to deal with the fact of our own mortality. And if we will, we have the opportunity to contemplate the Cross and the meaning of One who suffered on our behalf.

O'Connor says that sickness is "a place where there is no company." How perceptive. Loved ones can be *with us*, but they can't be *sick with us*. They can identify with us and experience our suffering vicariously, but only we can feel our pain.

So, sickness and suffering can become a wilderness experience, a time of enforced solitude when we can think about who we are and where we are headed, about our values and our priorities.

The Wilderness Speaks of Discipline

The wilderness is a metaphor. It is a place of struggle, a place of solitude, and of testing. The wilderness also speaks of discipline.

God allowed Moses to spend years in the wilderness tending his father-in-law's sheep so he would be prepared to hear God calling him to go and deliver His people. Jesus spent forty days in the wilderness, fighting the devil, defining His ministry, and solidifying His relationship with the Father. Paul spent three years in the desert before he came forth to be the great missionary evangelist that spread the gospel to the then-known world.

The wilderness speaks of discipline. And all of us need that. We need to discipline ourselves, to bring our appetites under the mastery of the Holy Spirit, to get our priorities straight, to make sure that our focus is clear and that the source of our power is holy.

Someone has said that we don't buy a violin today and expect to give a concert in Carnegie Hall tomorrow. Similarly, we may be converted to Christ in a moment, but becoming a Christian, living and walking as a Christian, requires discipline and is a lifelong undertaking. As Christians we do not emerge from our conversion fully grown; we must grow. And we grow by discipline.

That young minister about whom I spoke would not have fallen had he been disciplined in his commitment, had he been willing to yield every area of his life to the lordship of Christ.

Those young couples whose marriages are threatened by adultery would not be where they are if they were disciplined in their sexual passions, if they were disciplined in giving themselves in sacrificial love to their mates in marriage.

Much of our failure, most of the sin of our lives, and a great deal of the pain and shame and estrangement we experience are the results of failures in discipline.

One reason many of us are weak Christians, easily tempted, and tossed about by every new idea, every false wind of belief and practice that blows our way is that we simply aren't disciplined. We don't pray in a disciplined way. We don't study Scripture. We're not faithful in worship. We don't confer with and build core relationships with other Christians, who hold us accountable and assist us in discerning the way we should go. We don't seek to bring every facet of our lives under the lordship of Christ.

The wilderness becomes an important part of who we are, because there we must become more disciplined Christians.

Angels in the Wilderness

We need to remember that while Satan is always in the wilderness and while the wild beasts there frighten us with their eerie howls, the angels are also there. That's what Scripture says: "And the angels waited on Him." In the wilderness the Holy Spirit ministers to us and gives us the perspective and the strength to walk in the way God calls us to walk. The power and authority of the Christ who dwells in us by the power of the Holy Spirit will destroy the demonic forces in our world.

Early in his adult life, John Donne, the great English poet, was enmeshed in a destructive lifestyle. He was addicted to alcohol. He abused women. His life was one of debauchery, a shamble of immorality. He was on a downhill slide, and hell and destruction were inevitable. Then something happened.

He met Christ. He yielded his life to Christ, and Christ came into his life and saved him from that hellish downhill slide.

Donne became one of England's most eloquent preachers. He met a wonderful woman named Ann and became a loving and faithful husband to her. Then she died, and Donne went into a deep depression. But again he found himself under the loving, powerful control of Jesus Christ. Donne allowed the power of Christ to deliver him from his depression. As a result of that experience he wrote his famous *Holy Sonnets*. In the *Holy Sonnets*, he speaks to Christ and says, "Unless you enthrall me, I shall never be free. Nor ever chaste, unless you ravish me."[6]

So it is with all of us. When we are enthralled by the love and power of Christ, we are given the power to withstand all the wilderness experiences of our lives. We're given the strength and resources to be freed from the demons that would possess us.

We need to remember this as we look in this next chapter at the fact that the devil never leaves us alone.

The Devil at Noonday

3

I resolve to act with courage, but when even a small temptation comes, I am at once in a great strait. It is sometimes a very trifle, whence a great temptation arises.

Can you identify the source of this confession? It is from Thomas à Kempis, spiritual giant and author of the devotional classic *Imitation of Christ*.[1]

The account of Jesus' temptation experience was told in the New Testament by Matthew, Mark, and Luke. Mark's story was abbreviated sharply. Matthew's and Luke's versions were much the same. However, Luke's closing was very revealing: "When the devil had ended every temptation, he departed from Him until an opportune time" (Luke 4:13). The King James Version translated that, "he [the devil] departed from him for a season." J. B. Phillips translated it, "the devil . . . withdrew until his next opportunity." And the New English Bible had it, "and the devil departed, biding his time."

This passage from Luke painted a very challenging picture. The time of the specific testing of Jesus was over. Satan knew he had lost the battle. But please note: The devil had not given up. He withdrew only to await his next opportunity. Woven through the Gospels is a continuous thread of attacks by Satan. Here is an example from Mark:

> *And He began to teach them that the Son of Man must suffer many things, and be rejected by the elders and chief priests and scribes, and be killed, and after three days rise again. He spoke this word openly. Then Peter took Him aside and began to rebuke Him. But when He had turned around and looked at His disciples, He rebuked Peter, saying, "Get behind Me, Satan! For you are not mindful of the things of God, but the things of men." (Mark 8:31–33)*

Jesus knew the tempter was using Peter to dissuade Him from taking the way of the cross and providing our salvation. If we fail to recognize this continuous battle with Satan, we will not learn lessons from Jesus that will enable us to withstand the wiles of the evil one. Mark it down: We are never delivered from the threat of temptation. The nature of temptation changes, but the tempter is always looking for that more opportune time.

In the last of the three temptations of Jesus in the wilderness, the devil took Him to Jerusalem and placed Him on the pinnacle of the temple and said to Him, "If You are the Son of God, throw Yourself down from here"(Luke 4:9).

And then he (the devil) quoted Psalm 91, verses 11 and 12: "For He shall give His angels charge over you, / To keep you in all your ways. / In their hands they shall bear you up, / Lest you dash your foot against a stone."

Now, that Psalm was intended to assure us of God's protection. It began, "He who dwells in the secret place of the Most High / Shall abide under the shadow of the Almighty. / I will say of the LORD, 'He is my refuge and my fortress; / My God, in Him I will trust.'"

And then in verses five and six the psalmist talked about how God delivers:

> *You shall not be afraid of the terror by night,*
> *Nor of the arrow that flies by day,*
> *Nor of the pestilence that walks in darkness,*
> *Nor of the destruction that lays waste at noonday.*
> *(Ps. 91:5–6)*

The suggestion is that the devil doesn't always come in the night. He doesn't always come at three o'clock in the morning, when we sleeplessly replay in our minds the turmoil, the battles, and the resultant guilt and shame of the day. He doesn't always come in exposure to the temptation of the flesh: sexual gratification.

Sure there is the terror that comes by night, and the "pestilence that walks in darkness." And there are also those dramatic encounters that know no time frame; they are the arrows that fly by day. This psalm, however, also talked about "the destruction that lays waste at noonday." The wilderness may develop, as à Kempis said, in the midst of "a very trifle."[2] There are the temptations that come at noonday, that come in the ordinary times of our life. These temptations are the most subtle, the most difficult to recognize, and thus, perhaps, the ones to which many are most vulnerable.

Noonday Occasions of the Devil's Coming

James Stalker wrote, "One of the chief powers of temptation is the power of surprise. It comes when you are not looking for it; it comes from the person and the quarter you least suspect . . . no bell rings in the sky to give warning that the hour of destiny has come."[3] So we ask, What are some of the noonday occasions in which the tempter may be strong? When does temptation come?

Jesus' temptation came immediately after His baptism, an act of obedience to the will of God. And, following that act of obedience, Jesus was affirmed by God, anointed "My beloved Son, in whom I am well pleased."

It was immediately after that experience of overwhelming confirmation by God that Jesus entered His life-and-death struggle with Satan. Let that register solidly in our minds. Satan doesn't leave us alone because we are seeking to follow Christ. Those who are anointed by God, affirmed as

His children, are not strangers to temptation. In fact, there is a sense in which the demons intensify their onslaught when persons become serious about obeying God.

The devil doesn't have to spend much energy on those who are not serious about their discipleship. They are already in his corner. His work is focused on those who are seeking to break free from the kingdom of darkness and to walk in the light of the Lord. Richard C. Davis told about a man, Bob Childers, who was born and raised in the Blue Ridge Mountains. After completing his seminary education, he decided to go back to the place of his birth. After thirty years of fighting moonshiners, primitive Baptists (who opposed Sunday school), and illiteracy, he became discouraged. He and his family had been the recipients of death threats, rock throwings, and verbal abuse. Upon pouring out his soul to an elderly church member, she said, "The way I figure it, the Devil works harder against those who work harder for the Lord. The Devil don't bother with those sittin' still."[4]

I had a sad experience in the summer of 1993. I was speaking at a ministers' conference and inquired of a friend about John (not his real name), a young minister whose career I had been following for the last eight or ten years. I learned that John had just taken a leave of absence from the church. He had been appointed two years ago to a congregation that had been one of the leading churches in the state, served by some of the outstanding clergy of that area. Though still a strong church, it had fallen on tough times because of inadequate leadership, changing neighborhoods, and all those things that characterize many of today's inner-city churches. But in two years, under John's leadership, the church had been completely transformed. John is a powerful preacher, a charismatic leader in the truest sense of that word, and a caring, loving person whose ministry attracts people who are hurting and who are looking for direction. The church had become a dynamic, growing fellowship. The worship attendance had more than doubled in two years.

Then it happened. The bishop and the district superintendents received letters from a couple of women in the parish that this young man served before coming to his present appointment. The women shared painful stories of sexual indiscretions with their pastor. And so the young man was forced to withdraw from ministry, at least for a time, until he could get his life together.

Now, to be sure, we don't know the whole story, and we may never know it. What we do know is that this young man was successful. Everything was going his way. His ministry was being affirmed, and his gifts were being used.

The lesson in his story is this: Temptation and defeat often come to us when everything is going well. Sometimes even when we are at the pinnacle. You see, when we begin to think we can rely on our own power, we drop our guard. We grow lax in discipline. We no longer acknowledge our dependence on the Lord. At the pinnacle of success, when everything is going our way, the "noonday devil" is likely to strike.

But note this as well: Temptation also comes at the opposite times in our lives—the times when our lives are dull and we're going through a period of spiritual or emotional drought.

Let me focus briefly on two areas. First, our Christian commitment. How easy it is to doubt the reality of God and to question any experience that we might have had with Christ when we are going through a stagnant period in our spiritual growth. Some of the most attractive and diverting thoughts come during times like that, thoughts like these: *It was all an emotional experience. It was just a phase I was going through. It was real because I wanted it to be real. But why isn't it real now? There must have been nothing to it.* You've had thoughts like that, haven't you? I have. Such thinking is fodder for the devil's work.

How important it is to realize that God speaks to us through our memory! So, when we are in those dry periods, which are common to most of us, we need to exercise our memory and recall those occasions when we knew that Christ was present in our lives, working with us, leading us to paths of growth and maturity and service.

We need to be careful. We must be vigilant and watch out for temptation when we're in a period of dryness.

The second area in which we are vulnerable to temptation is in the area of sexual passion.

In my nearly forty years as a pastor, I have seen men fall into adulterous relationships at emotionally extreme periods in their lives—either when they were riding high in their professional success, or when their lives had become extremely dull and drab.

What I indicated earlier—that temptation and defeat can come when all is going well—is a fact that often comes to bear on the sexual indiscretions of very successful people. They think that they are a law unto themselves, that they can control things.

We are also vulnerable at the other extremes in our lives—when life is drab and boring. At those times, we are vulnerable to double-edged offers of excitement and pleasure, and sometimes we sacrifice fidelity and family and commitment for what we think is going to bring something new and fresh and transforming into our cold, drab, and empty lives.

This is the tempter's big lie. Screwtape, the worldly-wise old devil in C. S. Lewis's classic book, *The Screwtape Letters*, pens brisk, businesslike letters full of fiendishly clever advice to his young nephew, Wormwood, the tempter who is trying to lead people astray. In one of those letters, Screwtape said, "To get the man's soul and give him nothing in return—that is what gladdens our father's heart."[5] Remember, now, this was a demon speaking, and he was talking about the father of all evil when he talked about gladdening the father's heart.

And then he added that it is in the *troughs*, that is, in the low times, the drab, dull times, that the tempter should begin the process.[6]

How many times have I seen women enter adulterous relationships when their lives have become dull and boring, when their husbands had given them all the things that money could buy, but failed to give them their time and attention.

So, we must be vigilant. The devil comes at different times in our lives; he often comes when we least expect him.

Testing as Well as Temptation Comes at Noonday

Let's come at our subject from a different direction. The devil at noonday provides not only temptation, but testing as well.

The Epistle of James makes it clear that God doesn't tempt us.

> *Blessed is the man who endures temptation; for when he has been approved, he will receive the crown of life which the Lord has promised to those who love Him. Let no one say when he is tempted, "I am tempted by God"; for God cannot be tempted by evil, nor does He Himself tempt anyone. But each one is tempted when he is drawn away by his own desires and enticed. Then, when desire has*

conceived, it gives birth to sin; and sin, when it is full-grown, brings forth death. (James 1:12–15)

The key principle here is this: God does not allow temptation in order to threaten our faith, but to deepen it.

The words *tempt* and *temptation* are not used in the New Testament with uniform significance. Sometimes the words mean "to try" or "to prove." Sometimes they are used in the sense of "to lure" or "to seduce."

The Greek word used in the Gospels' account of Jesus' temptation is sometimes used to refer to experiences of sorrow, suffering, persecution, or deprivation—experiences that we as Christians must endure, and that, when used, can develop our moral character and enhance our spiritual strength.

But the word also refers to the enticement to sin in whatever form it may come. To be sure, it is temptation as enticement to sin that is dominant in the account of Jesus' encounter with Satan in the wilderness. Even so, we cannot overlook the fact that on this same occasion, Jesus was being tested. Register then this truth: *Every test is not a temptation, but every temptation is a test.* Let me explain.

We mentioned earlier the timing of this temptation in the life of Jesus. It came immediately after He was affirmed by God, anointed by Him as "My beloved Son in whom I am well pleased." But it is also important to note that the temptation came before Jesus launched His public ministry.

Could it have been that the devil was as much troubled by what lay ahead in Jesus' life and ministry as he was in what Jesus had already experienced in His baptism and anointing?

So, again, underscore it: *Every test is not a temptation, but every temptation is a test.* Both come, and they come frequently. And oftentimes, there is a thin line between the two.

Do you remember the story of Paul and his "thorn in the flesh"? We read in 2 Corinthians 12:7–10 that something painful and devastating was Paul's constant companion. Some have imagined it to be epilepsy; others, deteriorating eyesight that the harsh sun of the Middle East made especially vexing. We don't know what it was, but Paul prayed earnestly for deliverance from it. No deliverance came.

Paul gave us a challenging testimony and extraordinary insight. He called this "thorn in the flesh" a "messenger of Satan" from which he learned to "take pleasure." Why? Because it forced him to depend on the grace and power of Christ.

The noonday devil works by turning our testing into a temptation to fall away, to turn our back on the Lord, to become bitter and cynical and doubt the presence of Christ in our lives and in the world.

So we need to remember: Every test is not a temptation, but every temptation is a test.

Jesus Met Satan on the Ground of His Humanity

As we think of Jesus' temptation, we learn a great lesson by registering the fact that Jesus was tempted as a human being. He met the devil on the ground of His humanity.

Listen to how the story began. "Jesus, being filled with the Holy Spirit, returned from the Jordan and was led by the Spirit into the wilderness, being tempted for forty days by the devil" (Luke 4:1–2). The name at the beginning of that sentence and the name at the end are significant. Jesus was led by the Spirit into the wilderness to be tempted by the devil.

In his challenging study of Jesus' temptation experience, W. Graham Scroggie reminded us that the name *Jesus*, in connection with this temptation experience, was of great importance. It was not as the divine Son of God that He entered the wilderness. To be sure, He had been baptized and had heard the affirmation that God was pleased with Him, but it was as Jesus—the man—that He entered the wilderness. It was not as the Christ, the One whose name is above all names, but as Jesus, *fully human*, that He went to wrestle with the devil. It was not as the Lord—the One before whom every knee will bow and every tongue will confess to the glory of God—that He entered the wilderness. It was as *Jesus*— the name that identifies Him as human, that brings Him into sympathetic touch with us and announces His purpose to save—as man, not as God—that He entered the conflict.[7]

In two of the three temptations, Satan appealed to Jesus, "If You are the Son of God . . ."

> Jesus absolutely refused to be drawn onto that ground, not out of consideration for the devil, but for us. The whole value to us of the temptation consists in this fact; for had Christ fought out that battle on ground we could never occupy, and in a strength we do not possess, it could never have been said of him, "He was tempted in all points, like as we are, yet without sin"; neither, again "in that he himself hath suffered, being tempted, he is able to succor them that are tempted." That great battle was fought out and won by Jesus, not only as a necessary self-discipline in preparation for the mission upon which he was about to enter, but also as our representative and champion. This could not have been had he met the enemy on any ground other than that of his humanity. Had he met the devil as the Divine Son, he would have proved to be his Lord, but not our Deliverer.[8]

There is another important issue here. Jesus' temptation and conflicts played an important role in His identification with us. The writer of Hebrews vigorously asserts that "though He was a Son, yet He learned obedience by the things which He suffered" (Heb. 5:8). John Knox made the case clearly:

> That the son of God was thus tempted gives instruction to us that temptations, although they be ever so grievous and fearful, do not separate us from God's favor and mercy, but rather declare the great graces of God to pertain to us.[9]

When We Believe, We Need No Explanation

Somewhere along the way, I have heard this truth: When we believe, we need no explanation; and when we do not believe, an explanation does not satisfy.

That's fitting to remember when we talk about temptation and the devil. Some people don't believe in the devil, or they seek to rationalize the experience of forces working against our best selves. As long as this is the case, the devil has us where he wants us. C. S. Lewis made the case delightfully and convincingly in one of his *Screwtape Letters*.

> My Dear Wormwood, I wonder you should ask me whether it is essential to keep the patient in ignorance of your own existence. That question, at least for the present phase of the struggle, has been answered for us by the High Command. Our policy, for the moment, is to conceal ourselves. Of course this has not always been so. We are really faced with a cruel dilemma. When the humans

disbelieve in our existence we lose all the pleasing results of direct terrorism and we make no magicians. On the other hand, when they believe in us, we cannot make them materialists and sceptics. At least, not yet. I have great hopes that we shall learn in due time how to emotionalise and mythologise their science to such an extent that what is, in effect, a belief in us, (though not under that name) will creep in while the human mind remains closed to belief in the Enemy. The "Life Force," the worship of sex, and some aspects of Psychoanalysis, may here prove useful. If once we can produce our perfect work—the Materialist Magician, the man, not using, but veritably worshipping, what he vaguely calls "Forces" while denying the existence of "spirits"—then the end of the war will be in sight. But in the meantime we must obey our orders. I do not think you will have much difficulty in keeping the patient in the dark. The fact the "devils" are predominantly comic figures in the modern imagination will help you. If any faint suspicion of your existence begins to arise in his mind, suggest to him a picture of something in red tights, and persuade him that since he cannot believe in that (it is an old textbook method of confusing them) he therefore cannot believe in you.[10]

After preaching a sermon on the devil, I received a letter from a woman in the congregation. The first sentence pulled me into the woman's witness:

51

I just wanted to affirm your boldness to preach on the devil and to "thank you" for "making public" a subject that many of us are too scared to talk about or too unsure of to accept—the truth of the reality of the devil and evil he vomits over the world.[11]

She went on to describe the fear that stalked her early years because of threats from her parents that if she was not good, the devil would get her. She told about being sexually abused as a child. She shared the story of when she was five years old, stumbling upon a cult ritual in her aunt's garage, where older children were mutilating a cat and chanting as they formed a circle.

They bound me and put me in the center tormenting and violating and ridiculing as older children do to younger ones. I was warned that, if I told, the same thing as the cat was receiving would happen to me and the devil would get me for telling.[12]

She talked about her recovery from addiction and how the demon of deception and denial worked overtime to force her relapse. She closed her letter with this word:

It's good to be able to finally write this and tell "another human being." But this letter would not be complete without giving God the glory for the transformation in my healing journey. For this happened only by the Healing Power of Jesus Christ. Just as Paul said, "It's not I that live, but Christ that lives in me." He has all authority here!!! and He has already defeated the enemy. [13]

Will you remember that? The noonday devil will keep returning. He will bide his time for another opportunity. But the power is yours to resist, to overcome, to defeat him in every encounter. The power? Christ in you!

Taking Care
of Number One

4

In his book, Invitation to Pilgrimage, *John Bailey wrote, "I am sure the bit of road that most requires to be illuminated is the point where it forks."*[1]

He's right. There is no place on our life journey where we need more light than at a crucial fork in the road, where we have to make a decision about which direction we are going to go.

Let's revisit what we have considered in the first three chapters. In the first chapter, "Is Your Devil Too Small?" we presented three truths: One, the devil is real; two, the devil is a personal power; and three, the devil wants to control our lives.

In the second chapter we looked at the wilderness as a backdrop for struggle. It's a place of solitude, where we are tested. It is also suggestive of our need for discipline. It demands clear thinking and committed energy. To cope in the wilderness we need all our resources.

In the third chapter, we focused on the text from Luke 4:13, the concluding words of the temptation account: "When the devil had ended every temptation, he departed from Him until an opportune time." This specific testing of Jesus was over. Satan had lost his battle, and he knew it. But the devil had not given up. He withdrew only to await his next opportunity.

We are never permanently delivered from the threat of temptation. The nature of temptation merely changes. The tempter bides his time, looking for his next opportunity.

That's where we have been thus far. We have presented, in a general way, truths about the power of Satan, the nature of sin and evil, and the shape and form of temptation. Now we narrow our focus and look at each of the temptations of Jesus.

Jesus' first temptation was to take care of number one, and to express His identity. "If You are the Son of God," the devil said to Jesus, "prove it." Interestingly, as indicated in Chapter 1, this particular temptation expression recurred in Jesus' life when He was going through the torment of crucifixion.

Likewise the chief priests also, mocking with the scribes and elders, said, "He saved others; Himself He cannot save. If He is the King of Israel, let Him now come down from the cross, and we will believe Him. He trusted in God; let Him deliver Him now if He will have Him; for He said, 'I am the Son of God.'" Even the robbers who were crucified with Him reviled Him with the same thing. (Matt. 27:41–44)

We are likewise tempted: *Prove it*. And we
fall into the tempter's snare, believing that our
worth is in what we know, what we produce,
how well we perform, what we have, how successful we are.
And we feel compelled to make sure others know these great
things about us. Henri Nouwen put it this way:

> We make ourselves believe that we are called to be
> productive, successful, and effective individuals whose
> words and actions show that working for the kingdom is
> at least as dignified an occupation as working for General
> Electric, Mobil, Digital, or the U.S. Government.[2]

As a minister, I have given in to the temptation that
Henri Nouwen warned about. We need to know that such
self-assertion, such identity expression, is a point where the
devil can most powerfully work.

Before we pursue that line of thought, let's take a little
side trip to explore an important aspect of the text. Satan is
striking a blow at the Incarnation. He is tempting Jesus to act
as the Son of God, not as a God-enabled person.

Let me remind you of one of the most beautiful passages
of Scripture, as well as one of the most descriptive passages
about who Jesus was. We find it in Paul's letter to the
Philippians:

> *Christ Jesus, who, being in the form of God, did not*
> *consider it robbery to be equal with God, but made Himself*

of no reputation, taking the form of a bondservant, and coming in the likeness of men. And being found in appearance as a man, He humbled Himself and became obedient to the point of death, even the death of the cross. (Phil. 2:5–8)

In daring Him to act as "the Son of God," the devil was asking Jesus to lay aside the Incarnation, to disregard His humanity. But Jesus refused to do that. He knew that His identity as a human being was essential to His purpose for coming into the world—to provide our salvation.

That's what the writer of the Hebrews was trying to tell us about the Incarnation, about why it was absolutely necessary for God to come to us as a man. So, we have that writer to the Hebrews saying, "Therefore he had to become like his brothers and sisters in every respect, so that he might be a merciful and faithful high priest in the service of God, to make a sacrifice of atonement for the sins of the people. Because he himself was tested by what he suffered, he is able to help those who are being tested" (Heb. 2:17–18 NRSV).

That's the reason the Nicene Creed emphasized the nature of Jesus Christ as *very God* and *very man*.

Don't ever get the idea that you are going somewhere that Jesus has not been, that you are tempted in a way that Jesus was not tempted, that you are suffering in a way that Jesus could not understand. He became like us. He was tested so that He could help us bear our testing. He suffered so that He could provide comfort for us in our suffering.

David Gooding gave a marvelous commentary on these two verses from Hebrews 2. He talked about how incredible it was: Jesus voluntarily sacrificed His equality with God to become like us. He was not forced to do it. He certainly was not obliged to do it. He did it willingly. He became our High Priest, offering Himself as the sacrifice to become the atonement for our sins. By allowing Himself to be tempted, He both understood what it was like and showed us how to resist it. Jesus not only became human, He allowed Himself to be born into poverty. Most of us have far more than He ever had. He did this in order to identify with suffering humanity and to be accessible to its humblest citizens.

And then Jesus died for us.

> How can we keep from worshipping a Savior like that? Be ashamed of his manhood? Be ashamed of his sufferings? Be impatient with our own suffering for his sake? How could we be? His very suffering is his glory— and ours too; for it is the royal road by which he will bring redeemed mankind to their destiny of sharing universal dominion with God's perfect man.[3]

Now, let's come back to our main train of thought— looking at the first temptation of Jesus and applying it to our lives.

Balancing the Law of Liberty
and the Law of Love

Note first that the tightrope we walk as Christians requires balancing *the law of liberty*—the freedom to do as we please, and *the law of love*—the freedom that makes decisions based on and shaped by love.

The devil appealed to Jesus, as he does to us, to assert Himself, to express His identity: "If You are the Son of God . . ." Now there's nothing wrong with asserting ourselves. Albert Camus said, "To know one's self, one should assert one's self."[4] So there is nothing wrong with expressing our identity, and expressing our identity calls for assertion.

A few years ago, assertiveness training was a big thing. A lot of people, especially women, needed this training. Our culture has oppressed and marginalized women in so many ways that many women need to learn how to be more assertive. But when our primary intent is to look out for number one, and we spend our energy doing that, we are in trouble.

C. S. Lewis wrote, "We must picture hell as a state where everyone is perpetually concerned about his own dignity and advancement, where everyone has a grievance, and where everyone lives the deadly serious passions of envy, self-importance, and resentment."[5] The devil likes nothing more than to see us preoccupied with our own selves, our own rights and privileges, claiming our importance, and asserting our identity. The tight-

60

rope we walk, the big tension here, is between the law of liberty and the law of love.

There is no question about it: Jesus was the freest person who ever lived. He knew who He was, and He fought tenaciously and won over every temptation to deny His identity and His mission. But He didn't live by the law of liberty; He lived by the law of love. He would never make an unholy use of power. His use of power was always bound by love. He used power for love's sake. He would never use it to His own advantage if that brought harm to someone else, or if it meant taking from others their sense of self-worth, value, or self-esteem.

There's only one thing more costly than caring, and that is not caring. To be sure, love for others is demanding, often calling for sacrifice, but the alternatives are deadly.

We are experiencing the fallout of an era that has been labeled "the decade of me-ism." Self-absorption has been the driving force of our country. This is in direct opposition to the gospel Jesus preached. You remember His parable of the Last Judgment in the twenty-fifth chapter of Matthew. In that parable, Jesus paints a picture of some folks on the left, and some on the right; some to receive blessing, some to miss out; some to inherit the eternal reward of heaven, others to be cast into outer darkness. Jesus gives a simple basis for the difference in the judgment of those people. Their position, their destiny, was determined by their willingness to love or their failure to love. Those to receive the reward of eternal life were those who performed little acts of love and charity, simple expressions of caring: cups of cold water given in Jesus' name, kindness to a stranger, a visit to someone who was sick or in prison, caring for children, taking care of widows left without the support of a family.

I like the way Robert Raines defined hell:

> Hell is total preoccupation with self. Hell is the condition of being tone-deaf to the word of grace, blind to the presence of God, unable to discern his image in another person. Hell is that state in which we no longer catch the fragrance of life or breathe in the salt-breeze of the Holy Spirit; when the taste buds of life are so dulled that there is no tang or sparkle to living.
>
> Hell is to live in the presence of love and not know it, not feel it, not be warmed by it. It is to live in the Father's house like the older son (in the parable of the prodigal son) but be insensitive to the Father's love.
>
> Hell is to be unaware of God's world, God's people, the reality of God in one's self (to be spiritually blind); it is to have the doors of life closed tight to abide in one's own darkness.[6]

There is a law of liberty, and we do need to express ourselves. We do need to claim our own identity. We do need to assert ourselves. But remember, we walk a tightrope. The law of liberty must always be submissive to the law of love.

"I Want It—Now!"

Can you imagine His hunger? Jesus had been fasting for thirty-nine days. The Scripture says He was famished. So the devil hones in on Him. On the fortieth day, he taunts Him: "If You are the Son of God, command that these stones become bread" (Matt. 4:3).

This is the temptation to which we most often succumb—to satisfy immediate and pressing need. "I want it—and I want it now" is the theme song for too many of us. Jesus needed that bread, and there's nothing wrong with eating when we are hungry. But there was more than a loaf of bread at stake here. Was the story of Adam and Eve on Jesus' mind, when sin came into the world because Adam and Eve were tempted to eat the forbidden fruit? Was He thinking about the people of Israel wandering in the wilderness? God miraculously fed them with manna. But there were limitations to the manna. God put it out every day for a little while. They had to eat it then, and only then. They couldn't store it up for the future. Whether Jesus remembered those stories or not, He put the whole issue in perspective. He said to Satan, "Man shall not live by bread alone" (Matt. 4:4). He was not willing to give in to the feeling of the moment—no matter how urgent it seemed at the time.

The most cruel word for many of us is *wait*. Jesus could have used His messianic powers to satisfy His physical hunger—and the physical needs of all people. He resisted the temptation. He knew a deeper, spiritual hunger for God's love and power.

In the future He would make His claim: "I am the Bread of Life," sent down from heaven, not just to satisfy our immediate needs, but to satisfy our eternal hungers.

Likewise we are tempted to *satisfy immediate needs*—hunger, security, sex, acceptance, power. We try to accomplish God's purposes, to try to satisfy our eternal hunger with that which is only passing.

Could we learn a lesson from Elizabeth Taylor? If any contemporary, popular personality illustrates a lifestyle of giving in to the desires of the moment, it's Elizabeth Taylor. A few years ago, she wrote a book titled, *Elizabeth Takes Off*, and it turned out to be a best-seller. On the surface, it seemed to be a book offering advice on how to shed pounds by dieting. It was far more than that. The copy on the dust jacket explained its real message:

> ELIZABETH TAYLOR . . . GENEROUSLY SHARES WHAT SHE HAS LEARNED . . . TO ENCOURAGE OTHERS TO ACHIEVE THE RE-DOUBTABLE ENERGY THAT COMES WITH WINNING BACK YOUR SELF-ESTEEM.[7]

In the book, Taylor explained that the "winning-back process" started with a hard look at herself. As she looked into the mirror one morning, she saw not the beautiful star the world saw, or the talented, gifted person she thought she was; rather, she saw a woman who was destroying herself with drink, drugs, overindulgence, and unhealthy relationships. This was a devastating moment of truth for her, and she later wrote: "I had actually tossed away my self-respect. I had taken my image and scratched it with graffiti. I had thrown my gift away. . . . I was no longer even Elizabeth Taylor, the person I knew."[8]

That's what giving in to the desires of the moment does for us. It distorts who we are; in fact, it ultimately destroys us.

Nowhere do you see it more glaringly than in the arena of sex, or maybe I should say in the prevalence of sexual promiscuity. The statistics are shocking. Rare is the young person who gets out of high school without having had sexual intercourse. Too few people see fornication as the sin that it is.

Instant gratification and the diminished respect for the sacredness of the sexual relationship is creating havoc in America. The one-and-a-half million abortions in the United States annually are part of the painful harvest. The practice of homosexuality is another. The rising incidence of AIDS, which some are saying is moving toward epidemic proportions, is still another.

Then there's the high frequency of divorce. In my counseling I see it all the time. The sexual factor—the desire for instant gratification—causes infidelity and the shattering of relationships.

In our sexual morality, or lack thereof, we have sown to the wind and are reaping the whirlwind.

We see this in other areas of life. How we feel about and how we use money, the gifts we give our children, and the age at which we give them. (If you get your own car at age sixteen, what do you expect when you graduate from college? We turn our children into consumer addicts, and we grieve over what happens to them when materialism fails, when misfortune strikes and they aren't able to cope.)

Michael Lerner coined the phrase, "politics of meaning" in an article in *Tikkun* magazine in the summer of 1992. In that article he argued about the failure of liberals and moderates to understand America's hunger for meaning. Hillary Clinton used the phrase in one of her speeches. The media took issue with her and laughed Lerner onto the sidelines so that no one would take him seriously.

I mentioned earlier that the 1980s was the decade of me-ism. Lerner was saying that we dismissed that decade as a time of greed, when in actuality it was a decade of hunger—hunger for meaning in our lives. He has a valid point. It may well be that our drive to satisfy our urgent desires is the most telling sign of the lack of meaning in our lives.

Lerner made the point that we see clearly the problems of the have-nots—the jobless, moneyless, homeless, uninsured losers. What we miss, he adds, is that for many of us who are "winning the game . . . the prizes are less and less satisfying."

In his column in *The Commercial Appeal* on June 22, 1993, William Raspberry commented on this debate stimulated by Lerner:

> We strive for group advantage in the existing circumstances because we haven't figured out the need to change the circumstance. We chase money and privilege and exemption from responsibility because we haven't learned to identify the things we really hunger for.
>
> And when what we chase after doesn't ease the pangs, doesn't bring us any nearer to happiness—either as individuals or as a society—we chase all the harder after more of the same.[9]

So, I hope people like Michael Lerner will keep on talking. I wish there were a way we could find a "politics of meaning." In the meantime, recognize this important truth: In resisting the temptation to attain instant gratification, Jesus was pointing the way for all of us. None of us lives by bread alone. The satisfaction of our passions will never bring us meaning.

Go down the list:

- Sex
- Acquisition
- Pleasure
- Achievement
- Security
- Protection
- Pride
- Position

Taking care of number one is for many the undisciplined drive of their lives. Can anyone honestly say that the pursuit has brought meaning?

Bread That Does Not Satisfy

To hunger for food is natural. The passions of our humanity, our bodily appetites and natural cravings, are not sinful in and of themselves. But the tempter can use them to sidetrack us on our spiritual journey. He can use them to distort our identity, even to destroy us.

So, feeding ourselves is not wrong; indeed, it's natural and essential. The devil was asking Jesus to do the right thing for the wrong reason and at the wrong time.

Sooner or later, Jesus would satisfy His hunger. In fact, later on, He worked as great a miracle as He would have worked had He turned those stones into bread, when He turned five loaves and three fish into enough food to feed five thousand people. So it's not a matter of satisfying our appetites and passions, not a matter of responding to the deep longings of our soul. It's a question of when and why. It's a question of perspective and priority. It's also a question of understanding why bread alone will not satisfy. The urge to give in to the pressures and desires of the moment can be a deadly temptation.

Akin to this urge to succumb to desire is our effort to meet our needs in the wrong way.

We find a beautiful and challenging expression of this in Isaiah:

Ho! Everyone who thirsts,
Come to the waters;
And you who have no money,
Come, buy and eat.
Yes, come, buy wine and milk
Without money and without price.
Why do you spend money for what is not bread,
And your wages for what does not satisfy?
Listen carefully to Me, and eat what is good,
And let your soul delight itself in abundance.
(55:1–2)

Many of our needs are given and affirmed by God: hunger, sex, recognition, self-worth, relationships, intimacy, security. The psychologist Abraham Maslow has pictured our "pyramid of needs." At the base are our physiological needs: hunger, thirst, and sex drive. The second level includes our security needs: the need to feel comfortable, safe, and out of danger. The third level is the need for belonging and love—to be accepted and part of community. The fourth level is esteem needs: to achieve, to be competent, to gain approval and recognition. At the pinnacle of the pyramid is what Maslow called "self-actualization," the need to fulfill our unique potential.[10]

If we are to survive, live, and find meaning, these needs must be met. That is the reason we are so vulnerable to the devil's call to meet these needs in ways he suggests. When we fail to follow God's design in meeting these needs, or when we take shortcuts to meeting them, we are in spiritual peril.

The need for intimacy is a case in point. How many young people seek to satisfy their need for emotional closeness through sex? They, as many of their elders, mistake sex for intimacy. Intimacy has far more to do with honesty, trust, self-giving, a willingness to be vulnerable, than it does with sexual intercourse. Intimacy that builds relationships is a communing of spirits, not a joining of bodies.

So Jesus would teach us about the nature of marriage:

> But from the beginning of the creation, God "made them male and female." "For this reason a man shall leave his father and mother and be joined to his wife, and the two shall become one flesh"; so then they are no longer two, but one flesh. Therefore what God has joined together, let not man separate. (Mark 10:6–9)

It is not only in the area of our sexual drive and our need for intimacy, but also in all areas of life that Satan tempts us to opt for bread alone, for bread that does not satisfy.

Deny Dependence upon God

Let's move to another lesson that is here for us. The devil was tempting Jesus to doubt the providential care of God and

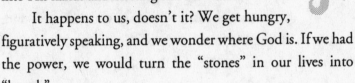

to deny His dependence upon God by taking matters into His hands and meeting His own needs.

It happens to us, doesn't it? We get hungry, figuratively speaking, and we wonder where God is. If we had the power, we would turn the "stones" in our lives into "bread."

When we lose our jobs.

When the bank balance runs low.

When a loved one is deathly ill.

When a son falls into the addiction trap.

When an unmarried daughter gets pregnant.

At times like these, we wonder, oh, how we wonder, where God is. And why He doesn't act. And why He doesn't deliver us. And the devil tempts us. "You do it. Turn those stones into bread. You can't depend on God."

And sometimes we respond to the lure of that temptation. We doubt the providential care of God and we try to go it alone.

Now here is the lesson: *We trust God for some things some times; we need to trust God for all things all the time.*

Abel Hendricks, a friend of mine, is a retired Methodist preacher in South Africa. He was the president of the Methodist Church in South Africa twice and was the recipient of the 1980 World Methodist Peace Prize. He and his wife Freda received the 1986 Upper Room Citation. They are among the most dedicated Christians I know.

Abel was jailed a number of times for his opposition to the evil system of apartheid and for his commitment to solidarity with the poor and the blacks of South Africa. In those days, he was identified by the government as "colored" which, in the oppressive social structure of apartheid in South Africa, was one step above the status of "blacks." South Africa is a nation whose political system, until recently, denied almost every basic human right to the vast majority of its population. Thank God, change has come to that land.

Years ago, before change came, Abel fought desperately against the system. In an effort to offer a morsel of appeasement, the South African government sought to establish two houses of parliament instead of an all-white house. One house would be for coloreds and one for Asians. Neither would have any ultimate power. Abel probably could have won a seat in the parliament of this new system. But his understanding of and commitment to the tremendous majority who would continue to be oppressed led him to oppose the proposed system.

In the midst of the struggle over the parliament, white leaders came to Abel urging him to rescind a pastoral letter he had written to the people of his district in which he urged them to boycott the election as an expression of love and solidarity with the poor and as a witness against apartheid.

The white government leaders thought they could get to Abel by appealing to his self-interest. He was not many years away from retirement and had no property of his own, so he faced an uncertain future. They offered him a retirement home, fully paid for, if he would simply "be quiet."

Hearing the offer, Abel smiled. I'm sure it was with one of the most disarming smiles the officials had ever seen, illuminating a face that resonated confidence and power as well as Christlike humility. "In my Father's house are many mansions," Abel said. "I dare not risk losing my house in heaven for anything you might offer me on earth."

What is the source of such clarity of conviction, such commitment to a people? Abel chose not to trust God for some things some of the time but to trust God for all things all the time.

His ministry became even more effective and his witness more powerful. He learned the lesson we need to learn; it's a lesson for us. God will never leave us nor forsake us. We may not understand His timing. His plan of deliverance may defy our logic. We certainly can't control His coming to us, either when or how He comes. But we can trust Him. We can depend on Him. We can know with Jesus that we do not live by bread alone.

Along with the temptation to deny our dependence upon God, there is in this temptation *an assault on authority*. In *Lord, I Can Resist Anything but Temptation*, Harold L. Bussell suggested that the devil was tempting Jesus to take control—to take authority into His own hands.

Satan did not say "Pray to the father that he would turn the stones into bread." Rather he said, "Command these stones." Isn't your power legitimate? Isn't your hunger legitimate? Isn't bread legitimate for meeting hunger needs? Isn't God, then, depriving you of legitimate wants? So whispers Satan in our ears.[11]

Jesus refused to fall for the trick. He would not take the authority that belonged to God into His own hands. How easily we lose the sense that all of life is a gift. We approach life as though it were entitled to us, something we earned or deserved.

Jesus' method of deflecting the devil's fiery dart is a lesson for us. The same Spirit who led Him into the conflict quickened His mind with a relevant passage of Scripture that exposed the insidious nature of the temptation. "It is written," Jesus said, "Man shall not live by bread alone, but by every word that proceeds from the mouth of God" (Matt. 4:4). These words expressed His complete confidence that His identity was in relation to the Father and that the Father would supply His every need.

Review. Taking care of number one is playing into Satan's hands. So we need to remember these lessons:

- We walk a tightrope in balancing the law of liberty and the law of love.

- Giving in to the desires of the moment is a deadly temptation.
- We must guard against meeting our needs in the wrong way. There is bread that does not satisfy.
- When we begin to doubt the providential care of God, we must avoid reliance on our limited selves and our own resources, which are never adequate. Though we can't control the *when* and *how* of God's intervention in our lives, we can trust Him. So, instead of trusting God for some things sometimes, we need to trust God for all things all the time.

To Trust God Is Faith; To Tempt God Is Presumption

5

*I*n Death Valley, there is a *place known as Dante's View. From this location you can look down into the lowest spot in the United States, a depression in the earth two hundred feet below sea level called Black Water. But from Dante's View you can also look up to the highest peak in the United States, Mt. Whitney, rising to a height of 14,500 feet. In one direction you move to the lowest spot in the United States, in the other, to the highest. From Dante's View, only the traveler can decide which direction to turn.*

That was Jesus' position when He was in the wilderness. And that's the position in which we often find ourselves, having to decide which way to turn.

Making decisions about the direction of our lives calls for trust on our part, an act of faith. And sometimes, instead of faith, there is presumption. Indeed, to trust God is faith; to tempt God is presumption.

In the last chapter, we looked at the first temptation of Jesus. We said that this was a temptation to doubt, or distrust, the providential care of God. We put it this way: Some people trust God with some things some of the time, while the call is to trust God with everything all the time. If the first temptation was to put ourselves first and doubt the providence of God, that is to refuse to be dependent upon Him, then this second temptation is to express a false dependence. It is the sin of presumption.

I got the title of this chapter from the great evangelist, Charles Spurgeon. He said,

> It is a precious doctrine that the saints are saved, but it is a damnable inference from it that therefore they may live as they list [please]. God gives us liberty, not license, and while He gives us protection, He will not allow us presumption. To trust God is faith, to tempt God is presumption.[1]

Look at the first two temptations of Jesus to see how subtle Satan was. He did not limit himself to one line of assault. In his craftiness he adapted himself to the situation. Notice that the two temptations swing in opposite directions. In the first temptation, he told Jesus to take things into His own hands, to "turn these stones into bread." In the second temptation, he told Jesus to cast Himself from the temple so He could prove that the Father would take care of Him. The focus of this second temptation is Jesus' confidence in God. See how sly the tempter is? In Luke, chapter 4, we see that he buttressed his proposition with a quotation from Scripture

(Ps. 91:11–12). "He shall give His angels charge over you, / To keep you, . . . / In their hands they shall bear you up, / Lest you dash your foot against a stone." Jesus was challenged to demonstrate His faith in the Father by putting this promise to the test. The first temptation was to cease trusting God; the second was to presume in His trust. So in this chapter we underscore the truth: To trust God is faith; to tempt God is presumption.

The Temptation to Spiritual Pride

Put one way, this is the temptation to spiritual pride.

The story is told of a woman who went to her Roman Catholic priest to make confession. She was a homely woman, yet she said to her confessor: "My sin is the sin of pride. Every time I pass a mirror, I'm overcome by my own beauty."

The priest replied, "I wouldn't worry about it, my dear. That's no sin. It's just a mistake."

Few of us are free of pride-run-rampant. To be sure, there is healthy pride: pride in what we do and how we do it, pride in an accomplishment, pride in the accomplishments of our children. But can we doubt the fact that too often pride runs rampant and degenerates into sin? I think the most distasteful of all pride-gone-rampant is spiritual pride.

Paul in his letter to the Romans reminds us not to think more highly of ourselves than we ought to think (Rom. 12:3). Such thinking is made more ugly and certainly more dangerous if we presume that we are at a spiritual level beyond which we actually are, or at a spiritual level that sets us apart from other folks.

There is a story about the legendary coach, Vince Lombardi, who had a legendary ego. On one occasion he had gone through a long winning series and was riding high. He came in one night after having won a tough game that his wife had not been able to see. She was already asleep. When he got into bed, his cold feet touched her legs, awakening her, and she said, "My God, your feet are cold." He responded, "When I'm in bed, just call me Vince."

We may not be guilty of such inordinate arrogance and pride, but none of us is delivered from the possibility of spiritual pride. We see it in its most glaring form in the popular idolatry of celebrity worship. We will not soon forget the story of Jim Bakker. I remember Chuck Colson, director of Prison Fellowship, reminding an audience that Bakker's story contained the primary element of a classic Greek tragedy: a leading character trapped in his own web of sinfulness and arrogance.

Jim was raised in a modest Muskegan, Michigan, neighborhood. He was a poor student and said himself that he had an inferiority complex. He managed only three semesters of Bible college before he launched his own small-town revival circuit. When he was twenty-five, the puppet show he and his wife, Tammy, produced hit the big time on Christian television. Fame came fast from that point; money began to flow in. With that money Jim built palatial estates and gorgeous buildings with high-tech studios. He wore $1,000 suits and Rolex watches. He and Tammy reportedly air-conditioned their dog's kennel. They became jet-setters, and they cruised Palm Springs in leather-lined limousines. They were even courted by presidential candidates.

As Chuck Colson concluded, some spiritual giants like Mother Teresa may be immune to pride, but like most of us, Jim Bakker was not. He fell, and great was his fall. Countless people played a role in that fall. They put Jim Bakker on a pedestal. They inflated his pride.

Disgust is a mild word to describe the response of most people, and few of us have not expressed that kind of disgust with the likes of Jim Bakker. Yet, we need to examine ourselves. We are all vulnerable to spiritual pride. It is possible for our blessings to become our drawbacks. When confidence dulls our sensitivity to our conscience, we become sitting ducks for the tempter.

Remember Jesus' warning to Peter in the Garden of Gethsemane? He had taken Peter, James, and John there to share with them His agonizing struggle as He faced the Cross. The Savior left them behind as He went farther into the garden to pray. When He returned, He found them sleeping. He said to Peter, "Watch and pray, lest you enter into temptation. The spirit indeed is willing, but the flesh is weak" (Mark 14:38).

We need to guard against the temptation to spiritual pride.

Tempting Providence

Look at a second truth that we are taught by this temptation of Jesus. When Satan challenged Jesus to cast Himself from the temple and depend upon the Father to save Him, he was daring Jesus to tempt providence. It helps to picture the setting. The temple was on the top of Mount Zion. At one corner of the temple, Solomon's porch and the Royal Porch met. At that corner, there was a sheer drop of 450 feet into the Kedron Valley below. The Jewish historian Josephus said that "anyone looking down would be giddy, while his sight would not reach to such an immense depth." Satan's temptation suggests two possibilities. One, that Jesus would throw Himself from that corner of the temple into the rocky abyss and allow the angels to "bear Him up." He would be saved "on angels' wings." The other possibility is that Jesus would throw Himself from the pinnacle, or tower, of the temple into the courtyard below, which was a hub of activity. Religious people would be streaming about, and they would be impressed by this great display of God's power. This action of God on behalf of Jesus would demand the attention of all.

In either case, Jesus would have been testing God. Such testing is the sin of presumption.

Presuming on God's presence and power is a common sin. Recovering alcoholics can teach us here. They talk about how important it is in the recovery process to change playgrounds, playmates, and playthings. They have to do that because the temptation is too great, and they can't flirt with that kind of temptation and expect to be delivered. They know they cannot presume on God's presence and power; they have to be vigilant in resisting temptation by refusing to put themselves in places that would make the devil's attack so easy.

So, we need to recognize the difference between faith and presumption. Faith is trusting God. Presumption is tempting God, testing His sovereignty, His love.

Consider some specific expressions of presumption that tempt God. We tempt the Lord and are presumptuous rather than faithful when we sit back and do nothing, saying with a kind of pseudo trust, "I'll just let the Lord take care of it."

I see that sort of thing all the time in my counseling. People will come up against a thorny issue in life in which their direction is unclear. There doesn't seem to be a definitive yes or no, no easy answer to the current problem. And they simply give up and say, "I'll let the Lord decide. I'll wait on Him for an answer."

I don't want to diminish the importance of waiting on the Lord. But waiting on the Lord does not mean total passivity on our part. The Lord expects us to grapple with issues, to use the resources He has given us, to engage ourselves in Christian conferencing with others, seeking to discern His will. Discernment of God's will sometimes comes as we struggle, as we engage ourselves in the dilemma. Discernment often comes when we make a decision to act, confident only that we have made the best decision that we could make, not that it is altogether what the Lord would have us do. The truth is that sometimes we have to act on our best judgment, even though we are not certain it is what God would have us do. It is then, in the midst of action, that we discover the guidance of the Lord. Sometimes we have to step into the sea before the waters will be parted.

We must be careful. We must avoid the sin of presumption, doing nothing in the name of waiting on the Lord.

Then there is this presumption, what Jesus was referring to when He said, "You shall not tempt the LORD your God": wanting the Lord to prove Himself. I also see this all the time—people wanting the Lord to prove His presence, to prove His power, to prove His love. That temptation is tied into our being enamored with the spectacular.

It is not unusual to read stories in the newspaper about this kind of presumption. Parents refuse to allow their child to receive a blood transfusion, or a person dies from the bite of a rattlesnake received in a worship service. Those are dramatic stories that make the news. The less dramatic don't. I know people who are always "putting out fleeces" that call God to act. And there are many radio and television preachers who "make a living" admonishing listeners to prove God by claiming a particular promise.

We have to be careful that we don't tempt the Lord by asking Him to prove Himself. We are called to trust, not to tempt providence.

Abandon Common Sense

And now a final truth for us in this second temptation of Jesus. This really was a temptation to abandon common sense.

Here we walk a thin line. Many things are not accomplished for the kingdom because people are not willing to take risks. The excuse they offer is that taking risks defies common sense. Author Oswald Chambers warned us against *enthroning* common sense:

> If we are devoted to Jesus Christ we have nothing to do with what we meet, whether it is just or unjust. Jesus says—Go steadily on with what I have told you to do and I will guard your life. If you try to guard it yourself, you remove yourself from My deliverance. The most devout among us become atheistic in this connection; we do not believe God, we enthrone common sense and tack the name of God on to it. We do lean to our own understanding, instead of trusting God with all our hearts.[2]

One of the big problems we have, not only in dealing with Satan but also with anything *supernatural*, is that we are so controlled by rigid, rational thought that our minds will not allow us to accept something we cannot *understand*.

When our drive to understand is in control, we are unable to appropriate faith. This clinging to the rational, along with an overdeveloped drive to understand, robs us of our ability to trust God, to release ourselves to receive whatever He has for us, whether we understand it or not.

Knowing this, we excuse ourselves by being too *reasonable*, too bound by common sense.

We are walking a thin line here when we consider the fact that Satan was tempting Jesus to abandon common sense. There is some truth in the modern proverb: God is not going to do for you what you can do for yourself. The balance is in what an old saint told me was the secret of her life. "I pray as though everything depended on God; and I work as though everything depended on me."

Consider the whole matter of medicine and healing. Aren't we tempting and testing God when we refuse to use the skills of trained physicians and the medicines that have been discovered as remedies for our diseases? Aren't we being presumptuous when we refuse all the means at our disposal for the healing of our bodies and simply wait in prayer for God to heal?

Refusing to use the resources that God has made available to us is not trusting God, but tempting Him. Prayer is most effective (and we have every right to pray for a miracle) as we employ all the means that we have been given.

There is a story of a man who went to the doctor and the doctor told him, "I'm sure I have the answer to your problem." The man answered, "I certainly hope so, doctor. I should have come to you long ago."

The doctor inquired, "Where did you go before?"

"I went to the pharmacist," the man replied.

The doctor snidely remarked, "What foolish advice did he give you?"

The man responded, "He told me to come see you."

In short, when you need a doctor, go to a doctor. When you need the pharmacist, go to the pharmacist. We need to use all the resources that are available to us, and we certainly don't need to abandon common sense. So, we should pray as though everything depends on God, and work as though everything depends on us.

Of course, there are those occasions when only the Lord can do what needs to be done. At those times we come to Him without hesitation, because we have been obedient. We've used the gifts that He's given us, the resources He has made available, and now we need the power that only He can provide.

When we come in that fashion we are trusting, not tempting, the Lord.

We have named and warned against three temptations:

1. The temptation to spiritual pride
2. The temptation to tempt God—that is to challenge God to prove Himself
3. The temptation to abandon common sense

87

To trust God is faith; to tempt God is presumption. In this regard, note carefully Satan's use of Scripture in his temptation of Jesus. Look at Psalm 91:11–12:

For He shall give His angels charge over you,
To keep you in all your ways.
In their hands they shall bear you up,
Lest you dash your foot against a stone.

Now look at Matthew 4:6, the evil one's word to Jesus:

If You are the Son of God, throw Yourself down. For it is written: "He shall give His angels charge over you," and, "In their hands they shall bear you up, / Lest you dash your foot against a stone."

Do you see? The devil left out the phrase "*To keep you in all your ways.*" It is not a dramatic display of power that the psalmist is talking about. Nor does the context have anything to do with "claiming a scriptural promise" or "putting out a fleece" to prove God. The psalmist is saying that, provided we follow God's appointed ways, we are safe and cared for. His care is ongoing, not episodic.

The devil quotes Scripture for his own purpose, ignoring the context and disregarding accuracy. The way he quotes this passage from the psalmist destroys the original meaning. This passage does not teach the faithful to test God by asking

Him to act dramatically, or by taking unnecessary risks. Rather, it assures us that we are in God's sovereign care and are kept safe in His love wherever His way leads. Our attitude should be one of *yielding to* rather than one of *presuming on* God. Hannah Whitall Smith put this in clear perspective:

> In everyday religion there are three things that are always absolutely necessary in the attitude of the soul toward the Lord: to yield, trust, and obey. No peace, no victory, no communion are possible where these are absent; and no difficulty is insurmountable where they are present. It is a sort of universal recipe for the cure of all spiritual diseases and difficulties.
>
> To yield something means to give that thing to the care and keeping of another. To yield ourselves to the Lord, therefore, is to give entire possession and control of our being to Him. It means to abandon ourselves; to take hands off of ourselves.[3]

Jesus teaches us that it is only in this kind of yielding to the Lord that we trust God, yet not presume. Yielding to the Lord enables us to withstand any temptation of the devil.

Learning to Say Yes,
No, and Whoopee!

6

When Lesslie Newbigin was the Anglican Bishop of the Church of South India, he preached one day at the University of Edinburgh in Scotland. After the service was over, some students remained to ask him a few questions.

One of them said, "Bishop Newbigin, I didn't expect to hear such a provincial message from you this morning. You've traveled all over the world, you've lived in many different cultures, and yet all you talked about was Christ. Why didn't you bring some light from Mohammed or some inspiration from Buddha or some insight from the Upanishads?" And Newbigin looked at the young man and asked, "Are you a Muslim?" And the fellow replied, "No." "Well, then," asked Newbigin, "are you a Buddhist?" And again the young man replied, "No, I'm not." And then Newbigin queried, "If you're not a Muslim and not a Buddhist, what are you?" And the young man stammered around a moment and then said, "I don't know. I guess I'm supposed to be a Christian." And I like what Lesslie Newbigin said to him then. He said, "You know what, young man? If I were you, I wouldn't worry too much about Mohammed or about Buddha until I had made up my mind about Christ. *Depending on what you do with Him, your path in life will then take shape!*[1]

That's the ultimate issue for us Christians, and there can be no compromise. That's what the last temptation of Jesus is about. There is a heightening of the level of temptation as the devil works on Jesus. The pressure becomes more intense. W. Graham Scroggie reminded us:

> The appeal in the first temptation is to appetite. "Make these stones bread." In the second instance it is to adventure. "Throw yourself down and trust God." And the third instance is to ambition. "Worship me, and I will give you all the kingdoms of the world and their glory." The first was a temptation to doubt, the second was a temptation to presume, and the third the temptation to treason against God.[2]

At issue is the destructive potential of compromise. As much as anything else, we need to learn to say yes and no. In His Sermon on the Mount, Jesus, talking about the futile sin of swearing, urged us to be clear in our speaking. "Let your 'Yes' be 'Yes,' and your 'No,' 'No'" (Matt. 5:37). In 2 Corinthians, chapter 1, Paul answered accusations against him. People had accused him of vacillating, of wavering. Paul made his case with clarity and certainty (vv. 17–18): "Do I plan according to the flesh, that with me there should be Yes,

Yes, and No, No? But as God is faithful, our word to you was not Yes and No." And then he added one of the most powerful witnesses to who Jesus is:

> *For the Son of God, Jesus Christ, who was preached among you by us—by me, Silvanus, and Timothy—was not Yes and No, but in Him was Yes. For all the promises of God in Him are Yes, and in Him Amen, to the glory of God through us. (2 Cor. 1:19–20)*

Phillips translated this text as follows: "Jesus Christ, the Son of God . . . is himself no doubtful quantity, he is the divine 'Yes.' Every promise of God finds its affirmative in him, and through him can be said the final amen, to the glory of God."

The New English Bible translated it like this: "Jesus . . . was never a blend of Yes and No. With Him it was, and is, Yes. He is the Yes pronounced upon God's promises, every one of them. That is why when we give glory to God, it is through Christ Jesus that we say Amen."

As much as anything else, we need to learn to say yes and no. I like the way Willard Krabill puts it: "Those who are mentally and emotionally healthy are those who have learned when to say yes, when to say no, and when to say whoopee!"[3]

So this temptation deals with the ultimate compromise: Are we going to be faithful to God, or give ourselves to lesser gods?

Temptation to Power

Note first that this is a temptation to power, and where power is involved, compromise is always an issue.

Though writing about ministry and to ministers in particular, Henri Nouwen warned us all when he read from this temptation our "natural" drive for power:

> From the moment we present ourselves as the best representative of our grade school class to the moment we try to convince our country that we will be the best possible president, we convince ourselves that the striving for power and wanting to serve are the same. This fallacy is so deeply ingrained we rarely hesitate to reach for influential positions because we're certain that we do so for the good of the kingdom of God. What good can come from powerlessness? In this country of pioneers and self-made achievers, where ambition is praised from the first moment we enter school until we enter the competitive world of free enterprise, we cannot imagine that any good can come from giving up power and or not even desiring it.[4]

This last temptation was the most dangerous and glamorous of all. Get the scene clearly in mind. The devil took Jesus up on a mountain and showed Him all the kingdoms of the world. "All these things I will give You," he said, "if You will fall down and worship me" (Matt.

4:9). Luke recorded the devil as saying, "All this authority I will give You, and their glory" (4:6).

Authority and *glory*. What an offer. Certainly Jesus had a right to the authority, and certainly He was worthy of the glory. Yet He resisted. "Away with you, Satan! For it is written, 'You shall worship the LORD your God, and Him only you shall serve'" (Matt. 4:10).

The temptation to use power in distorted and destructive ways gets us on several different levels. Let's bring it down to where most of us live—our need to be in control.

This is an issue that has ramifications in the whole of life. It's not only a spiritual issue, but it is also an emotional issue. In fact, it is a primary mental health issue. It is a factor in the recovery of most addictions. It wreaks havoc in our families. Much of the conflict between husband and wife and most of the conflicts between parents and children swirl around our need to control.

Some women use sex to gain power. Some men abuse women sexually out of a sick need to control. In a newspaper survey, people were asked to name those things that made them happy. The number one answer was being in control.

As entire books have been written on the subject of power, we certainly can't deal with it adequately in one chapter. Let me narrow the focus and simply state the issue in a way that will get your attention and, perhaps, convince you to work on any of the same problems in your life.

For many of us the temptation to seek power, to gain control, expresses itself in two ways: one, the need to fix other people's problems, and two, the need to convince people to conform to our ideas and agendas for them.

When we give in to those temptations, when we try to fix other people's problems and convince other people to conform to our ideas and agendas for them, we are attempting to play God in their lives.

How often I have been guilty of this! With my children. With my wife. Too often, to those to whom we should be expressing love, we come across as someone who wants to control them. We need to remember that no one feels loved by someone who seeks to control them.

Frederick Buechner, an Episcopal priest and novelist, is one of my favorite writers. He also writes helpful books on the crucial issues of life and on theological understanding. In his book *Telling Secrets*, he wrote about the role that secrets play in the lives of families. He confessed his own pain and anguish in relation to an anorexic daughter. He felt helpless to do anything for her. He became aware of the fact that he was trying to control her rather than love her, and too many times he was acting out of his own need rather than out of concern for his daughter. Here is a part of his description of that experience:

My anorexic daughter was in danger of starving to death, and so was I. I wasn't living my own life anymore

because I was so caught up in hers. The only
way I knew to be a father was to take care of
her. . . . I didn't have the wisdom or the power
to make her well. None of us have the power to change
other human beings and it would be a terrible power if we
did. Everything I could think of to do or say only stiffened
her resolve to be free from, among other things, me. The
only way she could ever be well again was if and when she
freely chose to be. If your daughter is struggling for life in
a raging torrent, you do not save her by jumping into the
torrent with her which leads only to your both drowning
together. Instead you keep your feet on the dry bank, you
maintain the best and strongest of who you are and from
that solid ground reach out a rescuing hand.[5]

Certainly we want to help those we love when they are
hurting. But that's not easy. The worst thing we can do is to try
to fix their problems or convince them that if they would simply
conform to our own ideas and agendas, all would be well.

To resist this temptation to seize power, this need to
control, we've got to find the grace to let go of those we love. An
anonymous person wrote a poem about what it means to let go:

To let go doesn't mean to stop caring,
    it means I can't do it for someone else.
To let go is not to enable,
    but to allow learning from natural consequences.

To let go is to admit powerlessness,
  which means the outcome is not in my hands.
To let go is not to care for,
  but to care about.
To let go is not to fix,
To let go is not to be in the middle arranging
  outcomes,
  but to allow others to effect their own outcomes.
To let go is not to be protective,
  it is to permit another to face reality.
To let go is not to nag, scold, or argue,
  but to search out my own shortcomings
  and to correct them.
To let go is not to criticize and regulate anyone,
  but to try to become what I dream I can be.
To let go is not to regret the past,
  but to grow and live for the future.
To let go is to fear less and love more.[6]

There can be no compromise where the temptation to
seize power is concerned, especially in relation to others. Only
God deserves the place of control in the life of another person,
and certainly we need to note that His power is always defined
by His love. He gives us that love, offers us that grace in Jesus
Christ, and waits for us to come to our senses, to yield
ourselves to Him. Author Kenneth A. Schmidt provided a
clear challenge:

We must also discover and confess the faces of sin we wear with our families:

If we want to blame them because of hurts or neglect, we must confess our desire to be Controllers.

If we want to maintain our good image in their eyes more than we want to be God's children, we must confess our desire to be Rescuers.

If we desire their rescuing and support more than God's, we must confess playing the Victim role.

If we don't allow the Spirit to put these aspects of our old selves to death, they will continue to haunt us.[7]

If God can wait, if God can love and not control, He can give us the power to resist the temptation to control others.

Preserving Our Position

Another expression of control is *preserving our position*. The tempter corrupts our thinking and distorts our perception. He leads us to believe that our security is in what we achieve, the degree of success in our profession, the amount of money we have in the bank. "I will give you these kingdoms," he says to us. But *these kingdoms* are illusions.

I remember a thirty-two-year-old man whose life was broken because his success bubble had burst. He was a so-called "bond daddy," a bond salesman who had been a smashing success. It looked like a forever thing, with commissions soaring and the sky as the limit in his career. He bought a huge house and furnished it lavishly. His wife drove a luxury car, and he had a $62,000 sports car to play with. In the language of Perry County, Mississippi, he lived "high on the hog." Then the bottom fell out. He lost everything—house, cars, furniture, and his wife. I remember his pain and disillusionment. It took months of pastoral and psychological counseling to get him on solid ground again.

This is a dramatic example that is repeated over and over again, and many of these stories make the news—particularly when a victim commits suicide or, as in a recent case, the victim kills his wife and child, then shoots himself. But those dramatic cases are not the only instances in which the tempter does his devilish work. He leads us to believe

- that outward success determines our worth;
- that whom we know is more important than what we do;
- that appearance is the most important thing;
- that the end justifies the means;
- that we must make our decisions out of selfish interest, because if we don't take care of ourselves, no one will;
- that we must deny our failures and hide our weaknesses to maintain our image of strength;

- that we can forget the future because *survival now* is the name of the game;
- that we can use whatever power we have for our own sakes, because that's what power is for—to "feather our own nest";
- that if we don't dominate, we will be losers.

Expediency is one of Satan's guides to how we are to live, and one of his goals is *power*—to be in control. Not so with Jesus. Not only in His temptation in the wilderness but always, He refused to do the expedient thing, and He resisted every temptation to gain power over people. When He fed five thousand people with a few loaves and fishes, the enthusiastic crowds began a campaign to "make Him king" (John 6:15). Jesus, seeking solitude, escaped to the hills. From the beginning of His ministry until His death on the cross, Christ refused to give in to the lure of position and worldly success. Satan tempts us to give in to the natural drive for domination; Jesus calls us to serve others, to be humble and submissive, even to the point of sacrifice. It is only as we refuse to think more highly of ourselves than we ought to think, as Paul said, as we respond to Jesus' call to be servants of "the least of these" that we can be victors in the constant temptation to control and preserve our position.

Temptations to Choose Lesser Gods

Not only is this lost effort of Satan a temptation to seek power, it is also a temptation to choose lesser gods than our sovereign God, the Creator, the Father of our Lord Jesus Christ. This temptation raises the whole question of what we are willing to stand for and die for. There is truth in the general contention that "every person has a price."

Back in 1989, Ted Turner, the "Media King," suggested that the Ten Commandments were out-of-date. Cal Thomas, a news commentator, was inspired to respond:

> Move over, Donald Trump. Move over, Japan. You may think you're big time, buying up everything in sight, but Ted Turner has you beat. The man who has challenged NBC, CBS, and ABC by starting his own three-letter networks (CNN, TBS, and TNT) is now going after bigger fish. Ted Turner is attempting to take on God.
>
> Honestly, what could have gotten into the "mouth of the South"? In remarks before a group of broadcasters in Dallas, reported by the *Dallas Morning News*, Turner took on Christianity, which he called "a religion for losers." Turner said Christ should not have bothered dying on the cross. "I don't want anybody to die for me," he was quoted as saying. "I've had a few drinks and a few girl-friends, and if that's gonna put me in hell, then so be it."
>
> A few days ago, Turner spoke to newspaper executives in Atlanta. He told them that the Ten Commandments are out of date, kaput, expired. He said they need updating.

102

"When Moses went up on the mountain, there were no nuclear weapons. There was no problem with the ozone layer or these other problems." Turner wants to replace the Ten Commandments with his own version, which he calls the "Ten Voluntary Initiatives."

The first two Voluntary Initiatives are, "I love and respect planet Earth and all living things thereon, especially my fellow species, mankind." And, "I promise to treat all persons everywhere with dignity, respect, and friendliness."

Sorry, Ted. Your initiatives just don't have the same ring of authority as "I am the Lord thy God, which have brought thee out of the land of Egypt, out of the house of bondage. Thou shalt have no other gods before me." And, "Thou shalt not make unto thee any graven image, or any likeness of anything that is in heaven above, or that is in the earth beneath, or that is in the water under the earth."

As another Ted (Koppel) has said, "Our society finds Truth too strong a medicine to digest undiluted. In its purest form Truth is not a polite tap on the shoulder; it is a howling reproach. What Moses brought down from Mount Sinai were not the Ten Suggestions . . . they are commandments. *Are*, not were."[8]

Ted Turner's suggestion was bizarre. Few people would consider his "Initiatives" as a possibility, but many of us go a long, long way *implicitly* in doing what he suggests—disregarding God's sovereignty in our lives, substituting lesser gods for God, lesser laws for the royal law of love.

Consider the gravity of this temptation of Jesus. He was being offered the authority and the glory of all the kingdoms of the world. Graham Scroggie rightly reminded us:

> The bait in the first temptation was Christ's personal need. The bait in the second was the Jewish nation. "If you fall down and trust God the people will welcome you and acclaim you the long looked for Messiah." But the bait in the third [temptation] was the whole world. "All these things will I give Thee and the glory of them."[9]

We will never be tempted in this same fashion. But that does not mean the issue is not relevant to us. Do you remember Esau in the Old Testament? Out of hunger he sold his birthright for a bowl of soup. Do you remember Judas in the New Testament? He betrayed Jesus to His enemies for thirty pieces of silver.

More often than not, our temptations revolve around bowls of soup and pieces of silver.

How often do we allow what we perceive as physical or material needs to restrict our spiritual growth? How often do we obtain and use our pieces of silver inappropriately—spending more on vacations than we give to the poor, investing more in life insurance to secure our family when we die than we give for the spreading of the gospel to save others from eternal death?

Idolatry is defined as any nonabsolute value that becomes absolute and demands to be the center of a dedicated life. Satan's temptation to Jesus was to make power the final goal of His life. This power was represented in ownership, status, control, the esteem of others. The question for us is not whether status, money, power, success, position, or the esteem of others is inherently wrong or evil. The issue is our temptation to make them the ultimate goal of life. So, what's your price? What lesser gods are you allowing to take precedence over the eternal God of whom Jesus said in resisting temptation: "You shall worship the LORD your God, and Him only you shall serve" (Matt. 4:10).

Where Idolatry Leads

The temptation of Jesus was a temptation to seek power, a temptation to choose lesser gods, and thus it was all about compromise. Now consider this: It may be just another way of coming at the totality of the issue. This temptation is about boundaries.

Jesus was setting the boundaries: Are we going to give in to the temptation of power? Are we going to serve lesser gods and compromise our relationship to the eternal God? Again, I would like to get us on common ground and deal with a critical issue that is suggested here: Do we set boundaries? How are those boundaries defined? To what point will we go?

Many of the difficulties that we experience result from poorly defined personal boundaries. We may never have learned to say no to our parents, and we felt dominated by them. We may have never gone through the adolescent rebellion that established us as adults. Still others have said no so many times that they don't know how to say yes.

Let me give you a test to help you put in perspective the issue of boundaries and the difficulties that come to our lives as a result of not being able to set them.

How many of you have told yourself you have no right to say no?

How many of you have said with some degree of frequency, "I'm strong enough to sacrifice for someone else."

How many of you have welcomed the escape from responsibility by discarding your right to say yes or no?

I believe that not saying no when we needed to, or not saying yes when we wanted to, has led many of us into doctors' offices; it has put many of us in jail; it has caused some of us to lose our jobs and others to be divorced, and still others to live in destructive marriages.

Columnist Suzanne Fields wrote about this whole issue of boundaries in a column focusing on the brutality of young men in current culture. She was addressing the issue of increasing numbers of boys at ever younger ages who are sexually aggressive, violent, and vicious.

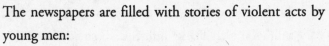

The atrocities committed by young men under age eighteen are epidemic, an increase of 85 percent in five years, according to the FBI. The newspapers are filled with stories of violent acts by young men:

Jennifer Ertman, 14, and Elizabeth Pena, 16, of Houston were raped repeatedly and then strangled with a belt and shoe laces. The suspects, six Houston teenagers ranging in age from 14 to 18 years old, stomped on the necks of the girls to make sure they were dead.

Playground sport now includes a recreational pastime called "pretending rape." A 12-year-old girl in Yonkers, N.Y., told police how eight boys, ages 9 to 13, threw her down on the ground and—while six other girls held her—aggressively fondled her. School officials told *The New York Times* that the boys had been "playing a rape game" that got out of hand.[10]

Ms. Fields reminded us that the experts blame the usual suspects—single parent families, television, movies, music, and advertisements that celebrate sex and violence and degrade women. But then she came to a disarming conclusion that I think is absolutely right. She said that it was also the fading of old-fashioned manners and the deterioration of traditional morals that have brought this harvest of violence.

There's something pervasively rotten in our personal cultural messages, too. For more than three decades we've mocked the ancient belief that men differ from women in their approach to morality, that women are "civilizing" influences on men, that male sexual aggressiveness requires informal as well as formal disciplines.

Manners and respectful gestures, such as opening car doors, a man standing when a woman enters the room, walking nearest the curb (where the water from the street splashes him, not her) and giving up a seat to a woman on a crowded bus are all gestures gone the way of fluffy pantaloons on piano legs. . . .

The code of the gentleman was the most successful extralegal mechanism ever devised for adapting male behavior to the requirements of modern life. . . .

The breakdown of manners and the destruction of traditional morals in bourgeois society knocked woman off her pedestal. Modern young men in groups are kicking her beyond recognition.[11]

In all of life we need boundaries. The devil whispers in our ears, "You are free. Don't let anybody tell you what to do. If it feels good do it. You deserve the pleasure." He knows full well that when there are no boundaries then life runs wild!

Whoopee!

We need to learn to say yes and no, but what about "whoopee"? Don't miss the conclusion of Jesus' temptation experience. The devil had tempted Jesus with three major allurements, and Jesus had won. Matthew closes the account, saying, "Then the devil left Him, and behold, angels came and ministered to Him" (4:11). Jesus sounded an unquestionable no: "Away with you, Satan!" He sounded a confident, triumphant yes: "Worship the LORD your God, and Him only you shall serve." And when that no and that yes had been sounded, then came the "whoopee!": The angels came and waited on Him.

It will be so with us when we resist these temptations. When we learn to say yes to God and no to Satan, then the "whoopee!" is inevitable. The form of the verb *ministered* in the Aramaic text is translated "kept on ministering." The angels ministered to Jesus as long as He needed them.

God's mercy does not spend itself in one act. God keeps on ministering to us. Divine reinforcements are always available in our times of temptation and testing.

What Lives in the Dark Grows in the Dark

7

On a November morn-ing in 1936, a man got up early, put on a pair of gray slacks and a maroon sweater, and entered the bedroom where his two young sons were playing games.

He then went downstairs to the garage, turned on the engine of the family Chevrolet, and sat down on the running board to await the exhaust fumes that would kill him.

There was no funeral, because neither the man's family nor his wife's family had any church connections. Funerals were not a part of the family's tradition. The body was cremated, and his ashes were buried in a cemetery in Brooklyn.

The man was the father of Frederick Buechner, author of *Telling Secrets*.

In recalling the death of his father, Buechner said he had no idea if anybody was present at the burial or not. He only knows that he, his mother, and his brother were not there. So Buechner concluded, "There was no funeral to mark his death and put a period at the end of the sentence that had been his life, and as far as I can remember, once he had died, my mother, brother, and I rarely talked about him much ever again, either to each other or to anybody else."[1]

The father's suicide became a "secret" that shaped that family to a marked degree. Nothing lends itself to the destructive work of testing and temptation more than how we handle secrets.

In previous chapters, we have focused on the experience of Jesus and how these particular temptations of Jesus in the wilderness express themselves in our lives. In this and the next two chapters, we will look at other temptations and testings that come to us.

A lot of temptation swirls around how we handle secrets. This is a testing experience, because how we handle secrets shapes us as persons and families.

Secrets: Sources of Sickness

Let's begin by simply underscoring the importance of secrets. Our secrets are not only part of our identity, they are often a source of our sickness, our dysfunction as persons and as families.

Buechner reflected on the suicide of his father, which was his family's secret:

Our secrets are not hid from God . . . but they are hid from each other, and some of them we so successfully hide even from ourselves that after a while we all but forget they exist. If somebody had asked me as a little boy of eight or nine, say, what my secrets were, I wonder if I would have thought to list among them a father who at parties drank himself into a self I could hardly recognize as my father, and a mother who in her rage could say such wild and scathing things to him that it made the very earth shake beneath my feet when I heard them, and a two-and-a-half years younger brother who for weeks at a time would refuse to get out of bed because bed, I suspect, was the only place he knew in the whole world where he felt safe. I knew that my father's suicide was a secret when that time came, but it was only a great deal later still that I realized that his life too had become a secret, almost the very fact that he had existed at all—the way he had looked and talked, the way it had felt to be with him, the way it had felt to be without him, back there at the start, before I had learned that the rule was that I was not to speak about such feelings and thus finally lost them to silence.[2]

Our secrets play a powerful role in the formation of our identities. They certainly play a powerful role in the dysfunction of families of alcoholics. Most alcoholic families have a rigid, unwritten rule: Don't talk about it.

No one talks about the problem to anyone else in or outside the family. The family, without making a deliberate decision to do so, closes ranks so that the secret will never be visible to anyone on the outside looking in. That's why sometimes when a family breaks down, and we discover that the cause of it is alcoholism, many folks who have been close to the family are surprised.

Secrets so shape the life of the family of an alcoholic that, more often than not, intervention is required. Someone has to break the secrecy syndrome and call for help.

Secrets and Bondage

Temptation and testing are always present in the way we handle secrets. We need to be aware of the destruction secrets work in our lives. Secrets are links in our chains to isolation, addiction, dependency, and codependency. Sometimes our secrets thwart our attempts to build wholesome relationships with others, even our redemptive relationship with Christ.

The power at work is primarily the power of shame. Our shame keeps us in bondage to our isolation, our dependency, our addiction, and codependency. It is like a fog that settles over our life, limiting our ability to see, certainly limiting our ability to feel.

This shame that we refuse to share with anyone else, that we try to keep secret, comes from several different sources: painful relationships, especially painful parental relationships; destructive habits that wreak havoc with those we love; failures and other painful past events; sick attachment to others, especially unhealthy sexual attachments. The list could go on. The shame grows, and the monumental question dominates our lives. "What if my wife . . . what if my

114

parents . . . what if my children . . . what if my friend . . . finds out the shameful person I am?"

Secrets paralyze us and keep us in bondage to isolation, dependency, addiction, and codependency.

We're as Sick as the Secrets We Keep

We keep deep, shame-inducing secrets locked away in the inner prisons of our souls. We are terrified to share these with anyone. They become like monsters that continually threaten us, working their destructive havoc in our life, keeping us on the edge of fear that someone will find out.

These unshared secrets tend to fester inside us. There is a sense in which we become as sick as the secrets we keep. In Matthew 15:18–20, Jesus said,

> But those things which proceed out of the mouth come from the heart, and they defile a man. For out of the heart proceed evil thoughts, murders, adulteries, fornications, thefts, false witness, blasphemies. These are the things which defile a man, but to eat with unwashed hands does not defile a man.

The Living Bible translates Mark 7:23, "All these vile things come from within; they are what pollute you and make you unfit for God." What happens is that our pain and emotions, all the secrets we not only fail to acknowledge to

God, but refuse to share with others, "spoil" within us. They pollute us, so we become as sick as the secrets we keep.

Kenneth A. Schmidt, in his book *Finding Your Way Home*, provided an analogy that enables us to visualize this truth: He asks us to imagine that after weeding our garden we put the weeds into a plastic bag, intending to throw them out with the trash. But we forget to get rid of the bag and after several months come upon it again. When we open the bag to see what is in it, we discover the rotting weeds. If we had put this material into a compost heap and let the air do its work, these same rotten weeds would have become fertilizer, which could have brought life to other plants.

Our suppressed emotions are like this, Schmidt says. If we keep them closed off within us, they fester and lead to diseased behavior and attitudes. We feel ashamed of them and don't let them "air out." We never learn to trust God about these things. We need to realize that the light that exposes our evil natures also cleanses us of them.[3]

After the death of Paul Tillich, it was revealed in a book by his widow that the famous theologian and noted seminary teacher had indulged in a wild and illicit sex life. When a teaching colleague was asked how it was that nobody at the seminary knew about this dark side of Tillich, he responded, "We all knew, and we refused to know that we knew." That's the kind of denial that makes us as sick as the secrets we keep. Satan uses this dynamic, making us fearful, fearful of what others might think if they knew, but also fearful of the pain that comes from *knowing*.

Parents see clear signs that their son is on drugs, but close their eyes. It would hurt too much to know.

A husband sees clear signals that his wife is having an affair, but shuts his eyes. It would hurt too much to know.

A salesman sees his commissions dwindling, yet continues his happy hour drinking, refusing to put the two together or admit that he is addicted. It would hurt too much to know.

Such self-deception is expressed in a myriad of ways. Lewis B. Smedes wrote this helpful thought on self-deception:

> What makes self-deception so hard to overcome is that we never consciously set out to deceive ourselves. A liar may get up in the morning and say, "I am not going to lie to my wife today." This is the double treachery of self-deception: First we deceive ourselves, and then we convince ourselves that we are not deceiving ourselves.
>
> Reality is flagging us down with red signals, blinking lights, beeping beepers, anything to get our attention. But, in a microsecond, we deny what we know and then we deny that we are denying it. Psychologists call this cognitive dissonance: the experience of having reality we do not want to know bang up against our minds while we deny its existence. "Don't upset me with truth I do not want to know."[4]

THE DEVIL AT NOONDAY

As long as Satan can keep us in a state of self-deception, he has done his job.

Some Secrets We Must Keep

With those reflections on the negative, destructive work of secrets, let me suggest a guide to living with and sharing secrets redemptively.

If it is true that we are as sick as the secrets we keep, then to get well, to know wholeness, we have to reveal our secrets, beginning, perhaps, by simply admitting them in our hearts.

There is a prayer in the liturgy of holy Communion that speaks to this issue:

> Almighty God, unto whom all hearts are open, all desires known, and from whom no secrets are hid: Cleanse the thoughts of our hearts by the inspiration of thy Holy Spirit, that we may perfectly love thee, and worthily magnify thy holy name; through Jesus Christ our Lord. Amen.

That's the beginning of living with and sharing secrets redemptively, knowing that God knows everything that we are. He already knows our secrets. He knows us thoroughly and loves us unconditionally.

Here are two specific guides for living with and sharing secrets redemptively. One, there are some secrets that you must keep. There are thoughts that we have, deep ponderings and internal struggles, that we may never need to share with another. There may be some past experiences that, if we shared them, would be destructive to another person or to a relationship. But remember, even those are known by God. The psalmist wrote, "O LORD, You have searched me and known me. / . . . Where can I go from Your Spirit? / Or where can I flee from Your presence? / If I ascend into heaven, You are there; / If I make my bed in hell, behold, You are there" (Ps. 139:1, 7–8).

Let me ask you. Do you really believe that all your secrets are laid bare before God? If you really believe that, do you find the fact frightening or encouraging? I hope you find it both frightening and encouraging. You see, there is nothing like the meaning that comes from growing in the intention of living our lives *Coram Deo*. Chuck Colson reminds us that that was the Latin cry of the reformers of the Protestant Reformation. *Coram Deo* meant "in the presence of God" or "before the eyes of God."[5]

I think this is a big part of what Scripture talks about when it talks about the fear of the Lord. When we live our lives *Coram Deo*, we live in the fear of the Lord, that is, in reverence and awe because of who God is. But we also live in hope, because we know what God desires of us, how much He loves us and wants us to know the wholeness, the joy, the peace, that can be ours.

What a marvelous position in which to be: to live our lives *Coram Deo*, that is, in the presence of God, in reverence and awe; but also to live our lives in the presence of God as the One Jesus addressed "Abba" or "Father."

In the Old Testament, God spoke from the mountain, He spoke from a cloud, and He spoke from His throne, as Isaiah experienced Him, "high and lifted up" (Isa. 6:1). To be sure, God made Himself known—visibly, audibly. But it would have never occurred to an Israelite to come boldly before the throne of God. God was the awesome and holy Sovereign.

But with the coming of Christ, and the God that we see in Jesus, an entirely new possibility between God and us was opened up. You see, with God as our loving heavenly Father, we have someone with whom we can share our deepest secrets.

J. I. Packer gave this superb explanation:

> What is a Christian? The question can be answered in many ways, but the richest answer I know is that a Christian is one who has God for his father. . . .
>
> The revelation to the believer that God is his father is in a sense the climax of the Bible, just as it was a final step in the revelatory process which the Bible records. . . . If you want to judge how well a person understands Christianity, find out how much he makes of the thought of being God's child, and having God as his father. If this is not the thought that prompts and controls his worship

and prayers and his whole outlook on life, it means that he does not understand Christianity very well at all. For everything that Christ taught, everything that makes the New Testament new, and better than the old; everything that is distinctively Christian as opposed to merely Jewish, is summed up in the knowledge of the fatherhood of God. "Father" is the Christian name for God.[6]

We can keep the secrets we need to keep, those that are connected with our identity, knowing that those are known by a God who knows us thoroughly and loves us completely, a God whom we may address as "Abba" or "Father."

That's the first truth to remember when you are tempted and tested with secrets: Know that there are some secrets that you must keep, but remember those secrets are known by God.

In the testing and temptation that come from our dealing with secrets, it is not enough to *know* that God knows. We must actively express our *knowing* that God knows. Satan would want nothing more than for us to forget the nature of God, or to grow dull in our awareness of God's love and forgiveness. We do forget and grow dull in our awareness if we fail to acknowledge and emulate God's nature in worship and prayer. One of the most powerful ways for doing this is confession.

Confession is the deliberate revealing of ourselves to God. This is essential not because we are informing God of something He doesn't know; He knows already. It is essential because it keeps us aware of God's love and grace. We cease denying our painful secrets, our crippling emotions and feelings of helplessness, and simply say, "Here I am, Lord. And here's my secret. I know You know, but I want You to know that I know You know. I am dependent upon Your love and grace, Your acceptance and forgiveness. I will not allow my shame and self-condemnation to blur my vision of You as my heavenly Father."

If there are some secrets that we must keep, we should remember that those secrets are known by God.

Two, everybody needs somebody with whom to share the secrets that need to be shared.

In the darkness, the mouse becomes the lion; in the light of revelation, the lion becomes the harmless mouse. Even the most dreadful secrets lose their power to frighten us when we say their names out loud, and what we share with others is not what drives them away, but what binds us to them, deepening the trusted relationship.[7]

If we have been imprisoned in shame, held bondage to some long-held, festering secret, we can let the sunshine in by simply telling someone about it. This is the last thing the devil wants us to do. His whisper fills us with fear: "Don't tell anybody. Can you really trust him? What is this going to do to your reputation? What if your friend tells someone else? No one needs to know. Just keep this to yourself." We must resist this temptation to remain silent.

The greatest gift we can give another person is the gift of ourselves. That is why intimacy in marriage is so important. Emotional intimacy is far more important than sexual intercourse in marriage. In truly intimate relationships, we reveal who we most deeply are. More marriages fail because of a lack of intimacy than for a lack of satisfying sexual relations. Indeed, much of the promiscuity we see today is an unknowing search for intimacy.

A department store advertised a new coat for women. The line was dubbed "casually yours." The ad boasted, "This coat captures beautifully the fine air of informal concern."

Informal concern—that's the mood of our day. We don't need to be "casually yours" to another person, nor do we need other people who will be "casually ours." We need people with whom we can share our life, whom we can trust, and who will receive our trust as a gift.

I saw the destructive power of secrets working in the life of a young woman in the church where I was serving as pastor. I also saw the powerful deliverance that can come when those secrets are shared with Christ, and with some significant others who love and care in an unconditional way.

This young woman had been sexually abused as a child by her father. Her deliverance came because of the patient, tender caring of two of the ministers on our staff with whom she was willing to share her secret. She broke from the cycle of violence in her family in her midteens. But for many years, she lived with guilt, shame, and depression, unable to free herself from destructive memories of that cruel violation.

She was under psychiatric care as well as pastoral care from ministers in our congregation. I noted that she always kept her distance from me. One day at a social reception, I walked up to her from the side, put my hand on her shoulder, and greeted her. She reacted in a very emotional way, and I knew that for some reason I had frightened her. She moved away from me as quickly as she could, without a word.

Later, one of the ministers on our staff who was counseling with her requested that he and this young woman come to see me together, and I learned the story. Somehow, because of a slight physical likeness, my presence triggered memories of her father and his violence. She confessed that she had dreams of her father's abuse, and in those dreams she would see my face. She had shared this only with her psychiatrist and pastoral counselor, and they had been working with her for months. It was amazing that even in the security of that room, with her pastoral counselor seated beside her, she had difficulty sharing that information in such close proximity to me.

I never will forget an experience about a month later. At our evening worship—which was a service of celebration, praise, holy Communion, and healing prayer—after receiving the sacrament, we invited people to come to the altar for specific prayer with one of the ministers. The ministers were on both sides of the chancel area, and usually people come to the minister nearest them. On this night, the young woman was seated on the opposite side from me, but at the time when we called folks to prayer, she almost ran across the front of the church and knelt before me. It was obvious that a power not her own was propelling her. She reached out to take my hands. Before that night, she would not have gotten within five feet of me. And she began to pray. Her prayer exorcised the spirits of shame and guilt and depression, the feelings of worthlessness and uncleanness that had come from being violated. The Holy Spirit prevailed over the negative emotions that had been ruling her life. The Spirit prevailed, because the love of Jesus Christ had been expressed through some pastors and an able and understanding therapist who cared for her.

That's dramatic, I know, but it can happen at every level of life.

When we know that there are some secrets that we are to keep to ourselves—they are a part of our identity;

- when we know that our secrets are known to God, and we live our lives in His presence;
- when we know that there are secrets that wreak havoc in our life, and the shame that comes from them renders us emotionally impotent;

- when we are willing to share those secrets with significant others and allow their love and acceptance to be a dynamic of healing and to represent the healing and restoration work of Christ;

then we can be free of the shame and guilt, the devastation of the shame of our secrets.

Let Not Thy Will Roar, When Thy Power Can But Whisper

8

Our chapter title comes from a quote by Thomas Fuller: "Let not thy will roar, when thy power can but whisper."[1] It's a challenging word, designating a common temptation: the temptation to be a victim. It happens to me, and I see it happening with persons around me. We desperately try to do something, to prove ourselves, to show that we have willpower and, more than willpower, the resources to bring to fruition what we will, when, in fact, we are weak. Our actual power is minimal. While our will is roaring, our power is whispering that we are not adequate, and that we are really fooling ourselves and trying to fool others. What is often the case is that we "roar," pretending to be strong when we actually see ourselves as victims.

The author of Psalm 109 clearly saw himself as the victim, and there is much of that throughout the Psalms. He painted a rather pitiful picture: "I fade away like an evening shadow; I am shaken off like a locust. / My knees give way . . . / my body is thin and gaunt. / I am an object of scorn to my accusers; / when they see me, they shake their heads" (vv. 23–25 NIV).

The whole nation of Israel adopted the victim mentality. This is reflected often in the Psalms. Here is an example of that:

You have given us up like sheep intended for food,
And have scattered us among the nations.
You sell Your people for next to nothing,
And are not enriched by selling them.

You make us a reproach to our neighbors,
A scorn and a derision to those all around us.
You make us a byword among the nations,
A shaking of the head among the peoples.
My dishonor is continually before me,
And the shame of my face has covered me,
Because of the voice of him who reproaches and reviles,
Because of the enemy and the avenger.
(44:11–16)

From ancient times until today, the temptation to be a victim rages.

There is a paradox here. A verse in Proverbs pictures an all-too-common stance: "Like clouds and wind without rain is one who boasts of a gift never given" (Prov. 25:14 NRSV). This supports the warning, "Let not thy will roar, when thy power can but whisper." To win over the temptation to be a victim requires balancing *will* and *power*.

The devil is always seeking to delude us into thinking we have power, that we can stand on our own. It began in the Garden of Eden. God had spoken clearly to Adam and Eve:

> *And the LORD God commanded the man, saying, "Of every tree of the garden you may freely eat; but of the tree of the knowledge of good and evil you shall not eat, for in the day that you eat of it you shall surely die." (Gen. 2:16–17)*

Satan spoke to Eve through the serpent: "Has God indeed said, 'You shall not eat of every tree of the garden'?" (Gen. 3:1). The account continued from there:

> *The woman said to the serpent, "We may eat the fruit of the trees of the garden; but of the fruit of the tree which is in the midst of the garden, God has said, 'You shall not eat it, nor shall you touch it, lest you die.'" Then the serpent said to the woman, "You will not surely die. For God knows that in the day you eat of it your eyes will be opened, and you will be like God, knowing good and evil." (Gen. 3:2–5)*

It was a temptation to gain power, but also a delusion that we have power that is not really ours. In our day-to-day life it expresses itself as self-will, cut off from dependence on the

Lord. And paradoxically, it often plunges us into a *victim mentality*, which pleases the devil no end.

Casting Ourselves as Losers

At a rather extreme level, many of us cast ourselves as losers. The psalmist was doing that: "I'm gone like a shadow at evening . . . my knees are weak . . . my body has become gaunt." And we do the same thing. Once we start playing the role of losers, we put ourselves in an ironic dilemma. It isn't that we can't find a solution to our problem. We can't see the problem.

The only way we are going to get a chance at a new role is to face up to the fact that our self-perception is at the heart of the problem, and that by perceiving ourselves as losers, we set the stage for defeat from the beginning.

Drowning Ourselves in Negative Thinking

Closely akin to casting ourselves as losers is a practice somewhat less extreme but still a dimension of the victim mentality: *drowning ourselves in negative thinking*.

Maxwell Maltz, the great plastic surgeon who was also a therapist and author of the classic book *Psycho Cybernetics*, said, "When a person drowns himself in negative thinking, he is committing an unspeakable crime against himself."[2]

Ponder that. We are committing an unspeakable crime against ourselves when we submerge ourselves in negative thinking.

I know people whose lives are ruled as compulsively by negative thoughts as those whose lives are ruled by addictions such as alcohol, drugs, or sex.

Our mind plays tricks on us. Satan uses the fact that the mind can be as irrational as it is rational to do us great harm. He works in our minds to give us feelings of power when we hold a gloomy outlook. Think about that for a moment. There is a sense in which we get feelings of power by holding a dismal and gloomy outlook. It sometimes expresses itself this way: "If I expect the worst, I won't be disappointed. If I think the worst about myself, no one else can cut me down."

This puts us in control and gives us power. If we have already put ourselves in a pit, no one else can put us there.

What happens is that when we drown ourselves in negative thinking, we deprive ourselves of the positive and pleasant aspects of life. Someone has suggested that it's like taking a drive and looking only at the garbage in the ditches, ignoring the beauty of the landscape beyond. What we see is real—the garbage *is* there—but it is a limited part of the picture.

In Herb Gardner's *A Thousand Clowns*, an uncle spoke of what he wanted for his nephew:

> I just want him to stay with me till I can be sure he won't turn into a Norman Nothing. I want to be sure he'll know when he's chickening out on himself. . . . I want him to stay awake and know who the phonies are, I want him

to know how to holler and put up an argument. I want a little guts to show before I let him go. I want to be sure before I let him go. I want to be sure he sees all the wild possibilities. . . . And I want him to know the subtle, sneaky, important reason he was born a human being and not a chair.[3]

This is the crux of it: We are not to be "Norman Nothings." To be a victim, to cast ourselves in the role of losers and drown ourselves in negative thinking, should be the farthest thing from beings created in the image of God. It should be the farthest thing from those who have claimed a saving relationship with Jesus Christ. The First Epistle of John said:

> *Behold what manner of love the Father has bestowed on us, that we should be called children of God! Therefore the world does not know us, because it did not know Him. Beloved, now we are children of God; and it has not yet been revealed what we shall be, but we know that when He is revealed, we shall be like Him, for we shall see Him as He is. (1 John 3:1–2)*

More often than we are aware, and to a degree greater than we realize, we cultivate the victim mentality. At an extreme level, we do this by casting ourselves as losers. Not so extreme but equally destructive is that we drown ourselves in negative thinking.

Unresolved and
Uncontrolled Anger

What is the psychological cause of a self-assumed victim mentality?

Very often, behind a self-assumed victim is a bundle of unresolved or uncontrolled anger. Those who study human personality and those who work professionally as counselors and therapists remind us that unresolved anger is often the source of low self-esteem. So, many times we adopt a victim mentality because we're angry and we lack self-esteem.

One of the primary sources of unresolved anger is a hurt that has been denied, mislabeled, or unrecognized. It doesn't matter who hurt us or when we were hurt or how we were hurt, if we don't recognize our pain, if we deny it, it becomes a hard core of anger. In fact, pain becomes more powerful when we refuse to recognize it or when we call it something else. To bury something does not mean that it is dead. It may simply mean that we have buried something alive that may eventually devour us from within.

My friend Jim Beaty recently told me a story about his father, Dr. Harold Beaty, my immediate predecessor as senior minister at Christ Church in Memphis and an avid golfer. On one occasion, at Chickasaw Country Club, Dr. Beaty was paired with a man he didn't know, an outstanding neurosurgeon in the city. This surgeon was known by everyone for his profanity. He could hardly speak three or four sentences without using foul language. He was especially known for cursing on the golf course.

Before the match started, someone told this doctor that Dr. Beaty was a preacher and that he should really guard his language. Well, the fellow tried to do so. He was disciplined in his speech. When they got to the seventh hole, the fellow had a magnificent drive, but on his second shot, which should have put him on the green, he sliced the ball and ended up in a sand trap to the right of the green. And he couldn't hold it any longer. He let out a long chain of profanity that would have made the proverbial "cursing sailor" blush.

Dr. Beaty didn't say a word, just looked at him. And the man turned red, shamefaced.

Four holes later, Dr. Beaty had been playing exceptionally well, almost perfectly. The tenth hole was five par. Dr. Beaty got off a long drive, was on the green with his second shot, and should have made the putt for two under par. It was an easy putt; anyone should have made it. But Dr. Beaty missed. He looked at his foulmouthed playing mate and said, "Would you please say something for me?"

Well, I would not want to come off as one who champions swearing, but I am a champion of expressing our anger. Unresolved or overcontrolled anger turns inward against ourselves, sometimes making us physically ill or depressed, sometimes bringing us to the point of hating ourselves, and almost always damaging our self-esteem.

Put another way: Behind the victim mentality is past pain that can undermine our current relationships. Some of our most painful experiences with others are the result of past experiences. For instance, we may deny ourselves an enriching relationship with a person who seems to want such a relationship because in the past we were smothered by a person who was constantly coming on strong, demanding more time and attention than we wanted to give. When we claimed some time and space for ourselves, the person lashed out at us, and severed the relationship. We don't want that to happen again.

Perhaps the most extreme and tragic expression of a victim mentality, in which past pain undermines current relationships, is sexual abuse.

In the last chapter, I told the story about the woman in our church who was sexually abused by her father; and who, through the power of the Holy Spirit and the instrumentality of two pastors in our congregation and a good therapist, was delivered from her shame and anger, delivered from a victim mentality. It happened because those two pastors and that therapist were patient with her, cultivated her trust, until she could run the risk of sharing the cause of her pain with them.

But before she was delivered, she suffered greatly and her current relationships were undermined. She struggled in her relationship to her husband and found it almost impossible to trust any man.

Expressions of Temptations to Be a Victim

Let's look briefly at sources of temptation to be victims. If we are aware of them, we can recognize them when the devil uses them.

The first is unrealistic expectations. When we begin to develop a victim mentality, we usually have unrealistic expectations of ourselves—and of others. We fail to realize that people come in many varieties, but *perfect* isn't one of them. We can be too demanding of others, and certainly too demanding of ourselves.

The devil makes no effort to be logical or consistent. If he can't turn you into a victim by convincing you to own unrealistic expectations, he seeks to lead you in a completely opposite direction—to convince you that you have no control over your life; that others may be able to practice self-control, but not you.

"I can't control myself" is the lie he plants in your mind. To the degree that you believe that lie, to that degree it will come true. You will find that you actually *can't* quit smoking or drinking or overeating. You *can't* resist whatever it is you want to resist. You *can't* do the thing you want most to do.

The *can't* is the lie that flows from the larger lie: "I can't control myself." As suggested earlier, the devil does his best work in our minds. As long as we declare that we can't control ourselves, we won't be able to.

Put the lie and truth in contrast. I know there are many

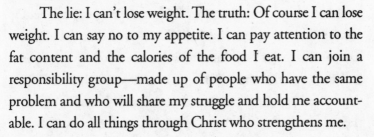

people who, because of genetic problems, cannot control their weight. But there are so many of us who have weight problems because we do not face the lie and the truth.

The lie: I can't lose weight. The truth: Of course I can lose weight. I can say no to my appetite. I can pay attention to the fat content and the calories of the food I eat. I can join a responsibility group—made up of people who have the same problem and who will share my struggle and hold me accountable. I can do all things through Christ who strengthens me.

Delusion and Denial

Let's consider how to deal with the temptation to be a victim. First, we simply need to face up to the truth about ourselves, our strengths, and our weaknesses. We have to stop playing general or chief operating officer, and become aware of our powerlessness in the face of certain circumstances.

Let me share my own experience. I grew up in severe poverty in Perry County, Mississippi. My mother and father did not go to high school. I saw myself as culturally, socially, intellectually, and economically deprived.

In reaction to that, I developed an almost "sick" determination to achieve, to get out of that situation, to be a success.

So I've spent a great part of my life driving myself unmercifully. The game I played was, "See here, I am worthy of your love and acceptance."

Throughout my life, until a few years ago, I had a recurring dream. I had to be somewhere to preach. The service was to begin in ten minutes, and I was struggling to button the top collar of my shirt, unable to do so, knowing that I was running out of time. Or I wasn't able to tie my tie. Or I discovered that the cleaners had mixed up my clothing, and I would put on a pair of pants and discover the coat didn't match, or even that the pants were three or four inches too short, or that I couldn't button them.

My anxiety expressed itself in all sorts of ways that demonstrated my struggle, my stress, my pressure, the drivenness of my life. All centered on my feelings of inadequacy and unpreparedness and the limitations of my past.

Well, I had not had that dream for a long, long, long time—many, many years. But on Tuesday night, July 27, 1993, the dream returned. Again, it was the same old thing. I had to preach at a great convention attended by a lot of people. I had not had time to make the kind of preparation I'm committed to making; I was just too busy. I kept saying to myself, "Well, undoubtedly, I'll get some time, and I can put something together." But time was not given, and the evening for my speaking came.

As I prepared to leave, I threw some sermon manuscripts into a file. Now this is interesting: I put the sermons into the kind of file my wife uses for her domestic work, an accordion-type file, usually brown, with ten or twelve compartments. I think that might have said something to me about being more dependent on Jerry, my wife. That's part of the answer to the temptation to be a victim. We need to accept the care of those who love us, to admit our need for that care.

I jumped in my car and headed for the convention hall. I got there fifteen minutes before it was time to preach, and I knew I had to be by myself and get some notes ready for my speech. I went into the first door that was available and found myself in a kind of canteen; there were chairs and tables and a counter. I sat down at a table and began to try to go through my file and find something that I could use that night.

I suddenly became aware that there were three women seated at a table in the room. I don't know where they came from, but they were there. One of them brought me a glass of milk. It was a kind gesture. The lesson: Life is not a competitive battle. We don't have to constantly prove ourselves. We can't live independently; we need each other.

Then I became aware that there were four men sitting at a table over in the corner of the room. One of them recognized me and came over and introduced himself as a minister. He told me he had been reading my books and using them in his church and that he appreciated my ministry. Instead of saying to him, "Look why don't we have some time together after the service tonight," I was very rude. I cut him off with some angry word about being interrupted.

The lesson: We can become so frazzled that we lose perspective, so involved that we can't discern priorities.

In desperation, I returned to my effort to prepare my sermon. Then it was time to go on, so I grabbed some notes and started to leave the room and go to the podium. I had on a freshly starched white shirt and my best suit—or I thought I did. I looked down and discovered I was wearing the pants of a jogging suit. The dream ended.

When I awoke at five o'clock in the morning, I was in a sweat, and I was worn out. I went to my study for my time of morning prayer after that dream. I felt I had received a message from God, a message to surrender, to let go.

I was the chair of the Committee on World Evangelism for the World Methodist Council, and I was supposed to leave that coming Sunday for two weeks to visit our congregations in the Czech Republic, to speak at a conference in Estonia, and to visit a congregation in Russia.

I was also chairing the Board of Trustees and the Search Committee to find a new president for Asbury Theological Seminary. That process was just getting under way and was a huge responsibility. I was working on a book manuscript that had a deadline four weeks later. A lot of things were going on in our church. We were growing and expanding in so many ways, adding new staff and planning building expansion. The opportunities for ministry were almost overwhelming. On top of all that, my mother had had a stroke the Sunday afternoon preceding the dream.

So God was speaking to me again, and on that Wednesday morning, I renewed my commitment to the Lord. I yielded to Him. I let go, and I let God. I canceled my trip to Russia. I said to the Lord that I was going to do my best to be a responsible chairperson for the Search Committee for Asbury, but I was not going to get all stressed out about it. I accepted the fact that it would not be catastrophic if I missed my book deadline. I would continue to be the best leader I could be for my congregation, but I was not going to carry the entire weight of it on my shoulders. God doesn't intend that for any of us. I committed my mother to the Lord.

So, I surrendered. My will, which may have been roaring, gave way to a whisper, because I realized again how limited I am and how dependent I am upon the Lord, how yielded I must be to Him if His power is going to be perfected in my weakness. The dream brought home to me the admonition: Let not your will roar when your power can but whisper.

The Perils of Our Passion for Security

9

*R*obert Morgan is serving now as the bishop of the Louisville Area of the United Methodist Church. Before moving to Louisville, he was bishop in Mississippi for eight years. About midway through his tenure in Mississippi, he suffered a serious heart attack.

During his recovery period, someone gave him a book by Dr. Robert S. Elliott, *Is It Worth Dying For?*[1] Bishop Morgan loves to talk about receiving the book and the message of it, saying that he wished somebody had given it to him twenty years ago.

Dr. Elliott gave two rules by which if we live, we will not have heart attacks:

> Rule #1: Don't sweat the small stuff.
> Rule #2: It's all small stuff.

Would that we could follow those rules. But most of us are not that healthy emotionally. Most of us are not that firmly established in our relationship to Christ. Few of us—perhaps none of us—are free from temptation and the testings that constantly come—testings that really threaten our very lives.

So, in this chapter, we look at an inviting temptation that really is a test—the temptation of security. We considered this briefly in Chapter 6. We now explore more fully the perils of our passion for security.

Renowned psychologist Abraham Maslow puts security in our hierarchy of needs. Security is a human need, and we are not going to be healthy and whole without a measure of security in our lives.

But that need can express itself neurotically. Satan can use it to throw us off the track of healthy living, but more than that, to throw us off the track of being faithful followers of Jesus Christ.

The need for security can become a passion, and that is a temptation we need to resist.

Confidence and Self-Esteem

The need to control can be an expression of a distorted need for security. See how this expresses itself in terms of confidence and self-esteem.

Security is connected with our confidence level, and our confidence level is connected with our self-esteem. It is seen rather clearly in the number of times we say "yes, *but*" to people in our lives. Consider the possibility that this evasive verbal stance is a concrete way to avoid revealing our lack of confidence, our feelings of inadequacy. Have you heard yourself saying recently, "Yes, but you don't understand my situation," or "I can't possibly do what you are suggesting. My case is so much more difficult than you realize"? Was the devil behind those "yes, but . . ." assertions? Was he feeding on your fear of change, your unwillingness to assume responsibility for your choice? Isn't it true that there is a connection between our measure of self-esteem and our level of confidence? Put another way, isn't it true that the primary ingredient of self-esteem is confidence?

One of the marks of confidence is being sure about what is going to happen, to be able to predict and control outcomes. Many of us reduce confidence to that primary meaning. Herein is a problem. We may know, or we may be able to reasonably guess, what is going to happen as a result of what we have done or what we see going on. We may be able to control some issues and events. But when it comes to the important questions in life, the big issues, we simply don't know.

As we begin to learn this, we move in another direction of seeking control. Then many of us look for security by *controlling as many other things as we can*. And that drives us to want to control relationships. We seek security by controlling our relationships. We looked at this in an earlier chapter when we addressed the issue of our relationships with our children. Do we do what we do out of genuine love or an inappropriate need to control?

Consider now a wider focus than parents relating to children. Psychologists have identified roles that people play in their attempts to control others, especially others in their families or intimate circle of relationships. They give names to persons who play a particular role in controlling. A common one is *scapegoats*. Scapegoats try to control others by misbehaving—yelling, cursing, whatever it takes to get attention. Anything is better than being ignored.

Another is *enabler*. We hear a lot about enablers from twelve-step programs. Enablers are classic controllers. They control by fixing other people's problems, keeping other people dependent upon them. Here is a simple clue to assist you in determining whether or not you are playing that role: Do you give advice when it isn't requested?

Enablers use a variety of methods to control people, by being devious in threatening others with rejection. Enablers are stingy with their praise. They use it only to enforce what they think is good—i.e., controllable—behavior.

Then, there is this interesting variation on the dynamic of controlling—the "lost child" method. The "lost child" is quiet and withdrawn in order to escape other people inflicting hurt upon him. Communication oftentimes carries the risk of additional pain, so the lost child avoids communication. This happens especially during stressful times. We close ourselves to others, even to the working of Christ, and are thus blinded to the options and possibilities we have. The more we focus on our worries and fears, the more our eyes are closed to any other possibility besides what we now see as

146

the only reality. The devil uses our fearful blindness to convince us that there is nothing we can do. He leads us one step further. He shows us how, even in our suffering, we are in control. By staying "lost," removed, outside the circle, the lost child is really controlling the relationship.[2]

There are other styles but this gives you enough to see what I'm talking about. None of these styles indicates real confidence. Rather, they all indicate a low level of self-esteem. Though not easy to recognize in ourselves, if we are really seeking wholeness, if we are serious in our Christian walk and believe that Christ can forgive and heal and restore, this is an issue with which we can deal. Christ can give us the confidence we need for self-esteem. Here is a thrilling statement of it:

> *Consider the incredible love that the Father has shown us in allowing us to be called "children of God"—and that is not just what we are called, but what we are. This explains why the world will no more recognise us than it recognised Christ. Here and now, my dear friends, we are God's children. We don't know what we shall become in the future. We only know that when he appears we shall be like him, for we shall see him as he is! (1 John 3:1–3* PHILLIPS)

If we could really believe that—that here and now we are God's children—then we would not have to control others to secure our identity, and we wouldn't have to have all the answers to be confident.

Underscore it: The need to control is an expression of a distorted need for security.

Deadly Caution

There is another expression of our distorted need for security: deadly, or extreme, caution.

I know people who have never gotten married because of their unwillingness to take risks. I don't know any relationship that provides a greater opportunity for us to grow than marriage. And growing always results in an increase in self-esteem.

Now, let me say immediately that I am not putting down the single life, nor am I being unsympathetic toward those who are single by circumstance, not by choice. But I want to make a case here for marriage and what marriage is all about by comparing it to the single life. I know that generalities do not express the whole truth, so I simply ask you to accept the limited but challenging truth of a comparison made by Earnie Larsen and Carol Hegarty:

> The single life can be a variable playground for false foibles, character defects, and general acting out of selfishness. When we are on our own, who is there to say, "Stop," "No," or "You can't do that around here"? Marriage provides a boundary within which wackiness of all kinds—

which would otherwise skip merrily on its way—gets confronted. In respectful, well-balanced marital relationships, we can't get away with the self-centeredness we don't even notice when we are alone. We are forced to listen better, share more, compromise fairly.

If we are married, we have profited from the responsibilities that may also have irritated us. Marriage is good for most people—not *in spite* of all its difficulties and demands, but because of them.[3]

If you refuse to get married because you are afraid of risk, you are missing a great opportunity for growth.

Procrastination

Control, deadly caution, and now, a third result of a distorted expression of our need for security: procrastination. Write that one large in your mind, because few of us are delivered from it.

Procrastination is a sign of fear. That's the reason we have to talk about it in the context of a passion for security.

How many times do we refuse to attempt something because of our fear of being unable to succeed at it? How many times do we spend endless hours of preparation, going over every minute detail, making sure that all the plans are in place and all the schedules are established? We sometimes use this as a delaying tactic because we are afraid to start. So, we procrastinate. Our procrastination is connected with our passion for security, and again, our need to control. It's a sign of fear.

In *Telling Yourself the Truth*, William Backus and Marie Chapian wrote a chapter entitled "Misbelief in Never Taking a Chance." They began as follows:

When people believe they should never take a chance, they commonly misbelieve a number of related lies, such as:

1. One of life's most crucial objectives is to prevent getting hurt. No matter what, I shouldn't get hurt.

2. Taking chances could lead to calamity. I could get hurt if I take chances in life.

3. Being safe is of utmost importance. It is terrible to be in any kind of danger.

4. It's terrible to make a wrong decision.

5. If I take chances in life, I could lose vital things like money, friends, approval, time, security.

6. I should never lose anything. Losing something is terrible.

7. I don't dare make mistakes. Mistakes are terrible.

8. I must always think ahead and try to foresee every possible trouble and woe.

9. I must intricately plan all of my actions as well as the

150

> words I say in order to prevent loss, pain, and disgrace.
> 10. God doesn't approve of risk-taking behavior.[4]

When I read that, I thought, *These are the lies Satan plants in our minds to feed our fears and to make us immobile.* When I find myself overly controlling, cautious, and procrastinating, I ask myself, "What is going on here? Is this an expression of my fear, my need to control? Is Satan the father of these lies?" I have learned that my procrastination is connected with my passion for security and is a sign of fear. It is not only a sign of fear as it relates to my *performance*, it also relates to my fear of rejection. We don't initiate relationships. We don't try for a new job. We don't express our ideas and feelings. We stay closed, imprisoned in ourselves, lonely and afraid, because of our fear of rejection.

All of us have a God-given need to love and be loved. Whether this need is met or neglected in our childhood shapes our emotional development.

> Some of us experience neglect, or a lack of bonding. Others experience unhealthy bonds with dominating, smothering, or abusive parents. Many face a baffling combination of these extremes.
>
> We want to be loved. We need to be loved. We try everything we can think of to experience love, but it is

151

elusive. Something is wrong, and we assume it is *us*. It's like we are standing at a water fountain. We are thirsty and want to drink, but our arms won't work to push the button to get the water to come out. We see others come up, drink, and go away satisfied—or so it seems. We try again, and again, and again. We are angry . . . ashamed . . . confused . . . and alone.

Or some of us may feel as if we're standing at a huge banquet table full of delicious-looking food. Our stomachs rumble from hunger, but we've eaten food like this before and it was poisoned. We are afraid. Others eat and survive. But we can't . . . there's too much risk of being poisoned again.[5]

I don't want to be trite about rejection, and I certainly don't want to appear as though I think it is easy. I know the depth of depression that comes to people who have been rejected. Many of us have been rejected so many times that we think that's the pattern of life. Somehow, some way, we've got to risk enough to know that rejection is not the norm. It certainly is not the norm in the Christian community. In that community, our identity is rooted in our relationship to God through Jesus Christ. In that community, we're aware that we are who we are by the grace of God, not by what we've accomplished, not by the position that we hold, but by the grace of God. *In a community like that, there is no place for rejection. Because we belong to Christ, we belong to each other.*

And the Church must work hard at seeing to it that a spirit of acceptance pervades the community of faith of which we are a part. In Galatians 3:28, Paul said it this way: We are one in Christ. There is neither Jew nor Greek, male or female, bond or free. He could have added, black or white, rich or poor, educated or uneducated.

Our Ultimate Security

We can withstand the devil's temptation to seek security in distorted and destructive ways by remembering that our ultimate security is in Jesus Christ.

To be sure, we need the security of food, shelter, family, relationships, and employment. That security keeps us alive and functioning as human beings, but even with those things, we can still be incomplete, unfulfilled.

Security comes from inside. It is rooted in our sense of self, our sense of identity, our sense of relationship with Jesus Christ and others. It's not dependent on circumstances. That means that even though the road may seem uncertain, *we* don't have to be uncertain.

In his first epistle, John reminded us that "We don't know what we will be in the future." When we are in relationship with Christ and that relationship is a *lively* and *working* one, then we know that life is more a *process* and a journey, than it is a matter of knowing answers and being in control. When we know where the road leads, we can be confident. It's when we don't know where the road leads that we are paralyzed with fear. So, John gave us reassurance: "What we will be has not yet been made known. But we know that when he appears, we shall be like him, for we shall see him as he is" (1 John 3:2 NIV).

If we cultivate our relationship with Christ, and if we have some friends who walk the road of life with us, then the road may be rocky and our way unclear, but we will not be frightened and insecure. We will not miss the lovely scenery along the way, nor will we fail to learn the lessons of the journey.

There is nothing wrong with being afraid, but to allow fear to paralyze us is out of keeping with our identity as children of God. "Behold what manner of love the Father has bestowed on us, that we should be called children of God!" (1 John 3:1); and that is not just what we are called, but who we are. When we keep our identity in relation to Christ intact, we are empowered, because we stay aware of the risk Jesus took on our behalf. He valued us, loved us, so much that He was willing to die on the cross for our salvation. If He was willing to die that we might be saved, He is not going to forsake us in the midst of life.

A letter I received from a university graduate student is a powerful witness to this fact. In it, a young man wrote about the ending of a special relationship that brought him almost unbearable pain. He describes it as "the kind that numbs someone, leads him to fear new relationships and allows this devil we oh-so-often deny to keep us still when our Lord would have us in motion." He talked about peers, who, not understanding the devilish complexities that have torn apart a relationship, ask "Why are you still single?" or say, "You should have no problem finding someone."

Here's an excerpt from his letter:

> Well, I found *someone* all right. His name is Jesus, and he does understand my longing to give of myself to others, though it is not money I'm able to give. He understands a rural-town boy who endures little indignities in a big city university for his desire to learn what they have to teach, yet apply it to a music that praises God and fills the soul. He understands someone who has been in a string of relationships with "significant others" who could not comprehend why I would do my utmost to love them just as they are—and left me because I was too close, gave too much, and stubbornly refused to understand why they would shut me out and leave. He understands someone who doesn't "circulate" very well in a crowded room, someone who sings a simple song for Jesus, someone who remains silent, when most others are speaking . . . He [Jesus] understands.

That says it, doesn't it? If we keep our relationship with Christ alive and growing, our identity and self-esteem will be secure in Him. Our passion for security will be a test, but a test that will strengthen rather than destroy. It will enable us to grow, because the temptation will keep reminding us that our ultimate security is in Jesus Christ.

I Saw Satan Fall

10

We have certainly not exhausted all the ways Satan seeks to control our lives. But perhaps our consideration has been enough to put you on guard, to sensitize you to the working of the evil one, who will lie, deceive, cajole, tempt, test, do everything to divert you from your commitment to and trust in Jesus Christ. But the devil does not have to win. We can share in the "fall of Satan." Indeed, we can live victorious over his efforts to control our lives._

In this final chapter, we will look at a dramatic word of Jesus about the "fall" of Satan, to see how we are to live in order to guarantee his continual fall.

The Devil Made Me Do It

We hear it all the time. We may have used it ourselves to excuse personal responsibility. "The devil made me do it." To recognize evil as a factor of life and Satan as a power with whom we must struggle doesn't let us off the hook.

Only recently has it come to me that one of Satan's smartest acts is giving us himself as an excuse. He takes it as a compliment when we say, "The devil made me do it." We will never win over temptation until we face it head-on, recognize it, and name it.

We considered earlier that the Greek word *pierasmos* may be translated "test," "trial" or "temptation." It is important that we not confuse trials with temptations. The Epistle of James helps us here:

> *My brethren, count it all joy when you fall into various trials, knowing that the testing of your faith produces patience. But let patience have its perfect work, that you may be perfect and complete, lacking nothing. If any of you lacks wisdom, let him ask of God, who gives to all liberally and without reproach, and it will be given to him. (1:2–5)*

The question is not whether trials will come. "When" not "if" you face trials, James said. Trials are inevitable. Their purpose is to produce endurance. But we must not confuse the issues. In the same passage, James talked about temptation being different from testing:

> *Let no one say when he is tempted, "I am tempted by God"; for God cannot be tempted by evil, nor does He Himself tempt anyone. But each one is tempted when he is drawn away by his own desires and enticed. Then, when desire has conceived, it gives birth to sin; and sin, when it is full-grown, brings forth death.*

Do not be deceived, my beloved brethren.
Every good gift and every perfect gift is from
above, and comes down from the Father of
lights, with whom there is no variation or shadow of
turning. Of His own will He brought us forth by the word
of truth, that we might be a kind of firstfruits of His
creatures. (1:13–18)

Not only are we not to blame our temptations and testings on God, as Christians we cannot *excuse* ourselves by blaming them on the devil. Temptations are a part of life, giving us opportunities to grow. If a Christian says, "The devil made me do it," he is admitting that he gave the devil more control than Christ. John Stott argues that the petition in the Lord's Prayer "deliver us from evil" should be rendered, "deliver us from the evil one." In other words, it is the devil who tempts God's people to sin; it is from him we need to be protected. These words that Jesus gave us to pray imply that the devil is too strong for us to resist unaided and that without God's help, we are too weak to stand up to him, but that our heavenly Father will deliver us if we call on Him.[1]

The battle centers in our will. Harold L. Bussell said it well: "Our wills are the taproots of our lives." They bring in God's nourishment. In order to keep this taproot strong, we must control our own attitudes. What goes on inside is most important. Attitudes shape actions. So God calls us to discipline our wills. We may have full knowledge of Scripture and

THE DEVIL AT NOONDAY

know what God would have us do, but without the will to pursue God's direction, our knowledge is useless. A disciplined will is essential in resisting temptation. Some people don't know what God expects and so they give in to temptation. Others get discouraged if they fall, while still others have difficulty strengthening their wills because of fear of failure. But the Word of God doesn't let us off that easily. The Bible teaches that our wills can and must be trained.[2]

Lewis B. Smedes, in his book *A Pretty Good Person*, addressed this issue of will and self-control in what he identifies as "hostile takeover" of our lives. He says, "We are shadowed by four forces that want to take over our lives. One is a *friendly* force; the second is a *necessary* force; the third is a *passive* force; and then, fourthly, there are downright *hostile* forces. We can lose control to them one at a time, or all at once."[3]

The *friendly* "takeover" force is *desire*. Desire is natural; it is a part of being human. If we lose desire we become numb, moving through life as robots. Yet, desire, out-of-control, is destructive. It is our desires that become addictions, and Satan uses our desires to his advantage.

Anger is another necessary force that Satan uses to color our lives and control us. This is the second takeover force. Like desire, anger has no control of its own. It can easily become a demonic fury. It certainly pleases Satan for anger to become blind and erupt into destructive turbulence, or to

160

burrow its way into our inner depths and become a burning resentment.

The third takeover force Smedes identified is *conformity*. This force has no passion, no rage, no ecstasy. Apathy slides us "straight into control by conformity," Smedes told us.[4] Satan relishes apathy. As long as he can keep us in this state, we are certainly no force for good, and no force against him.

These three takeover forces—desire, anger, and conformity—are, in turn, friendly, necessary, and passive. The fourth takeover force is outright hostile: It is the control of our life by Satan, the "prince of lies." Smedes concluded:

> What makes a demonic takeover a real threat to ordinary people is that we are seldom enticed to bargain away our souls, like Faust, in a single seduction. Evil whittles away, slicing a sliver here and a shaving there, getting us into the habit of making measly little compromises with deceit until we have vacated our control center and handed it over to the lie.[5]

We turn to Scripture, and to some of the most arresting words of Jesus. He had sent seventy-two disciples out to witness and heal. They returned to tell their stories, amazed at what had happened. Joyfully they exclaimed, "Lord, even the demons submit to us in your name." Then came Jesus' words: "I saw Satan fall." Read the entire passage:

After this the Lord appointed seventy-two others and sent them two by two ahead of him to every town and place where he was about to go. He told them, "The harvest is plentiful, but the workers are few. Ask the Lord of the harvest, therefore, to send out workers into his harvest field. Go! I am sending you out like lambs among wolves. Do not take a purse or bag or sandals; and do not greet anyone on the road.

"When you enter a house, first say, 'Peace to this house.' If a man of peace is there, your peace will rest on him; if not, it will return to you. Stay in that house, eating and drinking whatever they give you, for the worker deserves his wages. Do not move around from house to house.

"When you enter a town and are welcomed, eat what is set before you. Heal the sick who are there and tell them, 'The kingdom of God is near you.' But when you enter a town and are not welcomed, go into its streets and say, 'Even the dust of your town that sticks to our feet we wipe off against you. Yet be sure of this: The kingdom of God is near.' I tell you, it will be more bearable on that day for Sodom than for that town.

"Woe to you, Korazin! Woe to you, Bethsaida! For if the miracles that were performed in you had been performed in Tyre and Sidon, they would have repented long ago, sitting in sackcloth and ashes. But it will be more bearable for Tyre and Sidon at the judgment than for you. And you, Capernaum, will you be lifted up to the skies?

No, you will go down to the depths.

"He who listens to you listens to me; he who rejects you rejects me; but he who rejects me rejects him who sent me."

The seventy-two returned with joy and said, "Lord, even the demons submit to us in your name."

He replied, "I saw Satan fall like lightning from heaven. I have given you authority to trample on snakes and scorpions and to overcome all the power of the enemy; nothing will harm you. However, do not rejoice that the spirits submit to you, but rejoice that your names are written in heaven." (Luke 10:1–20 NIV)

Let's look at the ministry of the seventy-two for guidance to repel Satan's onslaught against us.

Satan Falls When a Person Trusts Jesus with His Life

Look at a part of the account of the seventy-two:

Go! I am sending you out like lambs among wolves. Do not take a purse or bag or sandals; and do not greet anyone on the road.

What trust! And that kind of trust is what made Satan fall. Jesus calls us to a radical trust. His tactic was to send His disciples out utterly defenseless, totally dependent on Him and on the reception of the people to whom He sent them.

They were to carry no cash, no spare clothes or provisions. Jesus was not only testing them, He had something else in mind as well. To be confronted by these servants of Christ, the people to whom they went would be forced to make a decision as to what they should do with them.

If the missionaries had enough money to support themselves, then letting them hire a room in a hotel would be a simple commercial transaction carrying no spiritual implication. But if the people were faced with penniless, destitute men, claiming to be Messiah's own ambassadors, they would be forced to decide whether they would receive and entertain them as such, or reject them.[6]

A preacher friend of mine told a story that speaks to us here. A pastor and his wife arrived at church a bit early for the evening activities one Sunday. They noticed one of the little girls of the church, perhaps seven or eight years old, sitting on the front steps with a big suitcase. The pastor's wife figured that the little girl had run away from home, so she went over and sat down beside her and began a conversation. A few general questions revealed that the little girl was not running away from home. "Well, why do you have this suitcase with you?" asked the pastor's wife. The little girl responded, "This morning the pastor asked who would follow Jesus wherever He went, and I said I would." She had come prepared.

William Manson spoke a challenging word concerning the nature of the Christian life. He said, "The life the Christian is called to live with Christ is not simply an improved version or expansion of the life of the past, but a contradiction of that former life."

Now the primary contradiction is that we cease trusting things and our own resources and we begin to trust Christ.

I remember visiting with a person in the hospital. He had had a close call. His recuperation was going to require a long time and much discipline. "It has been a saving experience," he said. "I have learned that I am not invincible." Then tears came to his eyes as he said, "I have confessed to God, and I want you to hear my confession also. I have trusted too much in myself and my money. I am praying every day that the Lord will forgive me, and I am seeking to put my total trust in Him."

I saw Satan fall in the hospital room that day, because Satan falls when a person trusts Christ with his life.

That same day, in the same hospital, as I was visiting some other patients, I heard the Harvey Team being paged. (The Harvey Team is a group of doctors, nurses, and technicians, ready to respond to an emergency, usually what appears to be imminent death.) It is a chilling experience to hear the alarm go off and see doctors and nurses run into the room where some person teeters on the border between life and death. I said a prayer for both the patient and the family, but I also reflected on my own life. Every time I try to die to self, the devil calls in his Harvey Team, and they work "like the devil" to keep the old man, the carnal man, the man who trusts in himself, alive. So it is an ongoing effort, a never-ending struggle—to deny ourselves, to cease trusting things and our own resources, and to trust Christ completely. But when we do that, Satan falls.

Satan Falls When a Person Stands Firm against Evil

Satan falls when a person stands firm against evil in whatever form evil may take. Look at Jesus' instruction to His disciples, as He sent them out:

> But whenever you enter a town and they do not welcome you, go out into its streets and say, "Even the dust of your town that clings to our feet, we wipe off in protest against you. Yet know this: the kingdom of God has come near." (Luke 10:10–11 NRSV)

Public action is called for from the church and from individual Christians. Winston Churchill was great with words. He was always able to put into brilliant succinctness expansive ideas and challenges. He said of the slow Allied response to Hitler's onslaught at the beginning of World War II, "Virtuous motives, trembled by inertia and timidity, are no match for armed and resolute weakness."[7] Satan falls when a person stands firm against evil in whatever form evil may take.

I remember an experience I had in China back in 1989. It was a few months after the demonstration in Tiananmen Square in which hundreds of thousands took a stand against the oppressive violation of human rights by the Chinese government. For "freedom fighters" in modern China, June 4, 1989, was a watershed day.

We were on our tour bus a few months later, and our guide, unsolicited, shared his witness. For me it was one of those Spirit-charged times—a *kairos* time, when history comes alive with God's presence and is shot through with meaning. We had seen dramatic pictures on TV—the square packed with a million people; students, holding high a replica of the Statue of Liberty, in juxtaposition to the huge poster of Chairman Mao as a statement about their desire for freedom; guns and tanks, pressing in on the protesters. And who can forget the picture of the courageous young man planting himself in the path of a tank?

Now we were hearing the story firsthand. I could hardly believe it. One of our guide's friends had been deliberately drowned by the authorities; another had both legs cut off. You can imagine the passion we heard in the words of our guide as he told us how important June 4 was and why, at great risk, he joined the students in Tiananmen Square. It was an even greater risk for him, because he worked for the government. I asked if he would get in trouble, speaking in this fashion. His answer was simple: "It doesn't matter, because what I'm saying is true. This is my conviction." He said that in the presence of a governmental official who, no doubt, was a party member.

Some of us wept; all were moved. I saw Satan fall that day, because Satan always falls when a person stands against evil, no matter what form evil takes. I also took courage that day, for my own life and witness. We do not have to be the victims of evil. As Tom Wright put it:

> It is the Christian claim that every square inch of the world, every split second of time, belongs to Jesus, by right of creation and by right of redeeming love. If we don't believe that, we are not following the Jesus of the New Testament. If we do believe it, we have no alternative but to find appropriate ways of expressing it. And the ways of expressing it will be both practical and symbolic. We must not underestimate the power of symbolic action; sometimes it speaks far louder than anything else.[8]

However we do it, we must take a stand against evil, and when we do, Satan falls.

Satan Falls When a Person Exercises the Power of Christ

Closely akin to a stand against evil is this dynamic: When a person exercises the power of Christ obediently,

Satan falls. Look at verses eight and nine of the account of the seventy-two:

> *Whenever you enter a town and its people*
> *welcome you, eat what is set before you; cure the sick who*
> *are there, and say to them, "The kingdom of God has come*
> *near to you." (Luke 10:8–9* NRSV*)*

Don't get hung up here with the ministry of healing, which Jesus obviously gave to His disciples. You don't have to jump off the deep end of the pool to get into the water. You can walk in from the shallow end. But to get in, you have to step or jump in somewhere.

My friend Leonard Sweet told me of the child who was the sole survivor when two great airliners collided in New York City some years ago. He had been thrown clear, landed in a snow bank deep enough to cushion his fall, and was then rushed to a nearby hospital. He was barely alive, however, because his body was so burned and broken. As he lay in the emergency room, he opened his eyes and looked into the smiling face of a nurse. She was a stranger to him, but the lad whispered to her, "I go to Sunday school." She responded with tears welling in her eyes, "Then you have come to the right place. God is here with you—and He and I are not going to leave you alone."[9]

We can get in that kind of pool, can't we? Making sure that where we are, God is. Making sure that we obey Christ by giving cups of cold water to the thirsty and feeding the hungry and visiting the sick and imprisoned. We can get in somewhere. And when we get in, taking a step of faith and attempting what we know we could never do in our own power alone, Satan will fall.

Satan Falls When a Person Is One with Christ

Satan falls when a person is so at one with Christ that Christ lives and acts through that person. Verse sixteen of the account said, "Whoever listens to you listens to me, and whoever rejects you rejects me, and whoever rejects me rejects the one who sent me" (Luke 10:16 NRSV).

That is a pretty clear picture of oneness with Christ, isn't it: "He who hears You hears Me, and he who rejects You rejects Me." But it is consistent with all of Jesus' teaching. You remember His metaphor of the vine and the branches in John 15:1–5, in which Jesus tells us who God is, and who He is in relation to God, and who we are in relation to Him:

> I am the true vine, and My Father is the vine-dresser. . . . I am the vine, you are the branches. He who abides in Me, and I in him, bears much fruit; for without Me you can do nothing.

Do you recall His petition in what we have come to call the High Priestly Prayer in John 17? Not the prayer He taught us to pray, but His own last anguishing prayer for His disciples and us. Give attention to His prayer:

> *I do not pray for these alone, but also for those who will believe in Me through their word; that they all may be one, as You, Father, are in Me, and I in You; that they also may be one in Us, that the world may believe that You sent Me. And the glory which You gave Me I have given them, that they may be one just as We are one: I in them, and You in Me; that they may be made perfect in one, and that the world may know that You have sent Me, and have loved them as You have loved Me. (vv. 20–23)*

"I in them, and You in Me . . . that the world may know that You have sent Me, and have loved them as You have loved Me." Satan falls when a person is so at one with Christ that Christ lives and acts through that person.

It was on the same visit to China to which I referred earlier that I met Pastor Kan at the Beijing Christian Church. Before the revolution in 1949, it had been the Asbury Methodist Church. For thirty years, no congregation was there. The building was used by the government for a school where atheism was taught and Christianity was scorned.

It was reopened as a church on Christmas Day, 1982. Every Sunday the church is packed with more than a thousand worshipers. At least four hundred attend prayer meeting on Wednesday night, and 1,300 new converts have been baptized over the past few months.

Pastor Kan was one of the ministers. He told of the oppression of the Cultural Revolution, the burning of Bibles and Christian literature, the destruction of churches—many turned into factories and warehouses—and the imprisonment of Christian leaders. Pastor Kan was banished to the countryside to work as a peasant laborer under primitive conditions. Many of his friends died. But here he was, thirty years later, now an old man, affirming the faithfulness of God with no trace of bitterness. His face glowed as it reflected the Spirit of Christ. His simple words were powerful. "God's grace is great. We must always be faithful." There was hope in his voice and firmness in his conviction as he concluded, "God holds our future in His hands. Tell our story to the Christians in America."

No wonder Satan had not completely prevailed in China. I saw him fall that day because Pastor Kan is so at one with Christ that Christ lives and acts through him.

An Attractive Door for Satan

Though it may seem to be a detour at this point of our consideration, I want to introduce a current attraction that Satan uses to seduce us away from the heart of the Christian faith and our life in Christ—the New Age movement. This movement is attractive to would-be Christians, to those who don't give careful attention to the substance of their belief and practice, and who naively believe that the content of the faith is not crucial. It is attractive to Christians of an activist orientation because it champions causes such as ecological responsibility and concern for creation, which rightfully are important Christian causes. We must see the movement for what it is. Tom Wright gave a succinct analysis:

> The theory behind New Age thinking is fundamentally astrological. The world, we are told, is moving out of the Judeo-Christian era, which is seen as the Age of Pisces. It is now moving into the New Age, the Age of Aquarius. Those who take this seriously—and they are increasing in number—believe that the transition in question, scheduled roughly for the turn of the millennium, is as important as the Renaissance or the Industrial Revolution, and will see a great change in Western society away from allegiance to the transcendent God of Judaism and Christianity and toward an Eastern-style monistic spirituality. Human beings will free themselves of transcendent deities and become conscious of their own inner divinity. This will be the age in which humans achieve a new status. They will become divine. (Wasn't this Adam and Eve's first temptation: "You shall be as God"?)
>
> There are many different phenomena in the current scene that can loosely be summarized under the phrase "New Age," and there are a great many people who have

been profoundly affected by the movement without actually giving it their explicit allegiance. But at its core the New Age movement has a clear history, a clear ideology, and a definite agenda. Its roots go back at least as far as the atheist philosopher Schopenhauer, and its pedigree includes the speculative theologian Teilhard de Chardin on the one hand and the composer Richard Wagner on the other. It also has links with influential theosophical and anthroposophical movements of some recent generations. It has given considerable impetus to various movements of modern witchcraft, notably Wiccan practices. In all these respects it is profoundly pagan, profoundly opposed to the traditional meaning of both Judaism and Christianity.[10]

Satan finds pleasure in raising the "attractive" aspects of the movement to seduce us away from the core of our faith and from the possibility of our being united with Christ. The New Age movement offers "self-fulfillment." Christianity offers fulfillment through "self-forgetfulness." In His resurrection, Jesus inaugurated the *real* New Age. And Christians—as they follow Jesus to the cross, forget themselves and their own selfish quest for fulfillment, find themselves bound to Christ through His forgiveness and love, and grow in their devotion to Him until Christ lives and acts through them—are a part of it. When that happens, Satan falls.

The world does not simply consist of one "impersonal

divine force" that human beings are to draw on in order to attain their own divinity, as New Age followers and other humanists would insist. Nor is evil simply a matter of people being out of touch with their own divinity. The forces of evil are not just "negative good" but principalities and powers with which we are called to do battle. Our calling is not to discover our own innate "divinity" but to receive the gift of God's own Spirit and His Son Jesus Christ to dwell in us and renew us, to make us "truly human," so that we might become one with Christ, and reflect His presence in the world.

Control

The ultimate issue is control. Who or what is going to control our lives? Many of us have traveled the long, hard road of self-control, thinking that with enough discipline and hard work, we could control ourselves. Self-control is essential, and we must be intentional and disciplined, giving vigilant attention to exercising our will against Satan and temptation. The ultimate issue of self-control is will, and the ultimate question is, To whom is our will surrendered?

The devil is real. The devil is a personal power who wants to control our lives. The raging center of the battle is our will. As we surrender our wills to Christ, Satan has no power over us. Never, never forget: "Greater is He that is within you than he that is in the world." Satan will always fall

- when we trust Jesus with our life;
- when we stand firm against evil;
- when we exercise the power of Christ, obediently in faith;
- and when we are so at one with Christ that Christ lives and acts through us.

Notes

Introduction

1. Thomas à Kempis, *Imitation of Christ* (Philadelphia: John C. Winston Co., n.d.), 144.

Chapter One

1. Maxie D. Dunnam, *The Communicator's Commentary,* Vol. 8 (Dallas: Word, 1982), 239.

2. J. Oswald Sanders, *Satan Is No Myth* (Chicago: Moody Press, 1975), 11.

3. M. Scott Peck, M.D., *People of the Lie* (New York: Simon and Schuster, 1983), 10.

4. Rob Johnson, "Satanic 'Dabblers' Can Become Deadly Disciples," *The Memphis Commercial Appeal*, 13 June 1993.

5. Peck, *People of the Lie*, 196.

6. Lewis B. Smedes, *A Pretty Good Person* (San Francisco: Harper and Row, 1990), 102.

7. W. Graham Scroggie, *Tested by Temptation* (Grand Rapids, Mich.: Kregel Publications, 1923), 10.

Chapter Two

1. Loren Eisley, *The Unexpected Universe* (New York: Harcourt, Brace and World, Inc., 1969), 27–28.
2. Quoted in *Touchstone: A Book of Daily Meditations for Men* (New York: Harper and Row, 1986), entry for 20 October.
3. Maxie Dunnam, *The Gospel of Mark* (Nashville: Cokesbury, 1988), 39.
4. Peck, *People of the Lie*, 42.
5. Flannery O'Connor, *The Habit of Being: Letters of Flannery O'Connor* (New York: Farrar, Straus and Giroux, 1979), 163.
6. John Donne, *Holy Sonnets* xiv, ll: 20–21.

Chapter Three

1. Thomas à Kempis, *Imitation of Christ*, 144.
2. Ibid.
3. James Stalker, *The World's Great Sermons* (London: Funk and Wagnalls), 171.
4. Richard C. Davis, *The Man Who Moved a Mountain* (Philadelphia: Fortress Press, 1970), 218.
5. C. S. Lewis, *The Screwtape Letters* (New York: Macmillan, 1962), 42.
6. Ibid., 37.
7. Scroggie, *Tested By Temptation*, 7.
8. Ibid., 7–8.

9. John Knox, *The World's Great Sermons* (New York: Funk and Wagnalls, 1908), 178.

10. Lewis, *The Screwtape Letters*, 32–33.

11. Letter to author.

12. Ibid.

13. Ibid.

Chapter Four

1. John Bailey, *Invitation to Pilgrimage* (New York: Charles Scribner's and Sons, 1942), 8.

2. Henri Nouwen, "The Wilderness Temptations of Ministry," *Leadership*, (Fall 1982): 62.

3. David Gooding, *An Unshakeable Kingdom* (Downer's Grove, Ill.: InterVarsity Press, 1989), 103–104.

4. Quoted in *Touchstone*, entry for 25 August.

5. Lewis, *The Screwtape Letters*, ix.

6. Robert Raines, *Reshaping the Christian Life* (New York: Harper and Row, 1964), 80.

7. Elizabeth Taylor, *Elizabeth Takes Off* (New York: Putnam, 1987), [from the cover].

8. Ibid., 48.

9. William Raspberry, *The Memphis Commercial Appeal*, 22 June 1993.

10. Richard R. Bootzin and Joan Ross Acocella, *Abnormal Psychology: Current Perspectives*, 4th ed. (New York: Random House, 1984), 84–85.

11. Harold L. Bussell, *Lord, I Can Resist Anything But Temptation* (Grand Rapids: Zondervan Publishing House, 1985), 39.

Chapter Five

1. Quoted by Scroggie, *Tested by Temptation*, 51.
2. Oswald Chambers, *My Utmost for His Highest* (New York: Dodd, Mead & Company, 1935), 179.
3. Hannah Whitall Smith, *Every-Day Religion: The Commonsense Teaching of the Bible* (London: James Nisbet and Co., Ltd., 1902), 36.

Chapter Six

1. Dr. Norman Neaves, "Have You Come to a Fork in the Road?" (sermon delivered at Church of the Servant, Oklahoma City, Okla., 8 April 1990).
2. Scroggie, *Tested by Temptation*, 61.
3. Quoted in *Touchstone*, entry for 7 July.
4. Nouwen, "The Wilderness Temptations of Ministry," 63.
5. Frederick Buechner, *Telling Secrets* (San Francisco: Harper, 1991), 25–27.
6. Quoted by Walter Gerber in "Breaking the Control Habit," (sermon delivered at Menlo Park Presbyterian Church, 22 February 1993).
7. Kenneth A. Schmidt, *Finding Your Way Home* (Ventura, Calif.: Regal Books, 1990), 152.
8. Cal Thomas, "Ted Turner tries to take on God,"

The Memphis Commercial Appeal, 6 November 1989.

9. Scroggie, *Tested by Temptation*, 61.

10. Suzanne Fields, "When Boys Will Be Brutal," *The Memphis Commercial Appeal*, 19 July 1993.

11. Ibid.

Chapter Seven

1. Buechner, *Telling Secrets*, 7.

2. Ibid., 73–74.

3. Schmidt, *Finding Your Way Home*, 143.

4. Smedes, *A Pretty Good Person*, 74.

5. Charles Colson, *The Body* (Dallas: Word, 1992), 36.

6. Gary Friesen, *Decision Making: The Will of God* (Portland, Ore.: Multnomah, 1980), 251.

7. Earnie Larsen and Carol L. Hegarty, *Believing in Myself: Daily Meditations for Healing and Building Self-Esteem* (New York: Prentice-Hall Parkside, 1991), entry for 22 June.

Chapter Eight

1. Larsen and Hegarty, *Believing in Myself*, entry for 10 January.

2. Quoted in *Touchstone*, entry for 14 September.

3. Quoted by Maxie Dunnam, *Be Your Whole Self* (Atlanta: Forum House, 1980), 63.

Chapter Nine

1. Dr. Robert S. Elliott, *Is It Worth Dying For?* (New York: Bantam Books, 1989).

2. These names of persons who play a particular role in control were suggested by Robert S. McGee and Pat Springle in their book, *Getting Unstuck* (Dallas: Word, 1992), 152.

3. Larsen and Hegarty, *Believing in Myself*, entry for 26 January.

4. William Backus and Marie Chapian, *Telling Yourself the Truth* (Minneapolis: Bethany House, 1985), 126.

5. McGee and Springle, *Getting Unstuck*, 44.

Chapter Ten

1. John R. W. Stott, *Christian Counter-Culture* (Downers Grove, Ill.: InterVarsity Press, 1978), 150.

2. Bussell, *Lord, I Can Resist Anything But Temptation*, 135–36.

3. Smedes, *A Pretty Good Person*, 96.

4. Ibid., 99.

5. Ibid., 102.

6. David Gooding, *According to Luke* (Leicester, England: InterVarsity Press, 1987), 197.

7. Winston Churchill, *The Gathering Storm* (Boston: Houghton Mifflin, 1986), 171.

8. Tom Wright, *Bringing the Church to the World* (Minneapolis: Bethany House, 1992), 158.

9. Story told by Leonard Sweet, United Theological Seminary, Dayton, Ohio, repeated by Donald Shelby, "Together, We Will," November 5, 1989.

10. Wright, *Bringing the Church to the World*, 76.

ABOUT THE AUTHOR

MAXIE DUNNAM has a pastor's heart. At the beginning of his ministry he organized and served three churches in Georgia, Mississippi, and California. He served as Director of the Upper Room Fellowship Department in Nashville for two years and then for seven years was World Editor of *The Upper Room*. Following that he went to Christ United Methodist Church in Memphis and served there as senior pastor for twelve years.

In 1989 Dr. Dunnam was inducted into evangelism's "Hall of Fame" by the Foundation for Evangelism as one of Forty Distinguished Evangelists of the Methodist world. He has received the Chair of Honor from the World Methodist Council (1991) and has just been named a Senior Editor of *Christianity Today*.

In 1994 he answered the call to the presidency of Asbury Theological Seminary. In his position there and as Chair of the Evangelism Committee of the World Methodist Council, he continues to work, preach, and write for the furtherance of the Kingdom.